REPORT WRITING FOR LAW ENFORCEMENT

- Police
- Corrections
- Parole
- Probation
- Private Investigations
- Security

2nd Edition

Designed and organized in an easy-to-read and understandable format, this book's multi-purpose design makes it ideal as an academy workbook, a college text, as well as a personal resource. Currently in use by many police academies and law enforcement related training institutions.

INCLUDES THE FOLLOWING TOPICS:

Note Taking · Interviewing Techniques · Report Writing Exercises
Examples of Improper Word Use · Essentials of Grammar and Spelling
Frequently Misspelled Words and Jargon Lists

Instructor's Test Guide Available Upon Request!

PROFESSIONAL DEVELOPMENT ★ ★ SERIES

S0-AYW-933

Joseph N. Davis

LawTech Publishing

LawTech Publishing Co., Ltd.

1060 Calle Cordillera, Ste. 105

San Clemente, CA 92673

1(949)498-4815   FAX: 1(949)498-4858

E-mail: ReportWriting@LawTechPublishing.com

Web site: www.LawTechPublishing.com

Comments and suggestions are welcome.

ISBN: 0-915905-74-4

ABOUT THIS BOOK

REPORT WRITING For Law Enforcement is organized to present appropriate English language information and report writing techniques in a format that can be used on a daily basis. This book is designed to be used in a variety of ways:

- As a workbook for basic academy or in-service report writing classes.

- As a textbook for college level public service report writing classes.

- As a resource for supervisors and officers to refer to for specific, correct report writing information.

An Instructor's Guide is available; contact the author or publisher for further information.

ABOUT THE AUTHOR

Joe Davis began teaching police officers in 1979, and in 1983 began teaching report writing in the basic academy for the Orange County (California) Sheriff's Department and Rancho Santiago College. Since then his teaching experience has grown to include supervision, leadership, and communications skills classes at Chapman University, Irvine Valley College and private seminars and consulting. He is also the author of the *Report Writing Survival Guide*, a field reference version of this book, and President of Davis and Associates, Educational Programs for Peace Officers. Joe retired as a Captain from the Orange Co. CA Sheriff's Department after nearly 30 years of service. He can be contacted at 1(800)427-8223, or at *www.JoeDavis.org*.

ACKNOWLEDGMENTS

REPORT WRITING CONCEPTS is the culmination of not just my experience, but those of my associates and close friends. Michele Laughlin, Gerry Meyer, and Barbara Frazee have supported my efforts, edited, proofread, suggested, and polished not only this book, but my classroom lectures too. For their efforts I'm forever grateful. Phil Johnson is not to be forgotten for his efforts with Michele and me to produce four report writing scenario tapes. Stan Jacquot provided creative ideas and hours of hard work for me when he was a basic academy tactical officer.

Most importantly, I would like to thank my wife, Patricia Ann and daughters Christy and Amy.

Joseph N. Davis
Author

CONTENTS

CONTENTS

Chapter 1

INTRODUCTION TO REPORT WRITING

DEFINITION OF A REPORT

A report is a document, written on a departmental form, and kept as a permanent record.

TYPES OF REPORTS

Arrest Report

Arrest reports factually record the circumstances leading to the arrest of a suspect for a specific crime. They include the probable cause for the stop, detention, arrest, and disposition of the suspect.

Clearance Report

Clearance or investigation reports document the disposition of a case. Depending on agency policy, the disposition may be arrest, identification of suspect without arrest, recovery of property, restitution, or filing a criminal complaint.

Crime Report

Crime reports document the facts of an event showing a crime occurred. The report must include the elements of the crime. It may include descriptions of suspects, property taken, evidence collected, property damage, and injuries sustained by the victim. The report usually includes information about the suspect's modus operandi.

Daily Activity Report

Daily activity reports or officer's logs are used to record the officer's activity. Typically the reports include the location and a brief description of the officer's activity.

Evidence Report

Evidence reports record the collection and preservation of physical evidence at a crime scene. They may also include a request for forensic examination and the result of that examination. Evidence reports document the chain of evidence.

Incident Report

Incident reports are sometimes called service or miscellaneous reports. They are used to record the facts of an event that isn't a crime. Typically, these incidents are medical aid calls and civil disputes.

Memorandums

Memos are reports written to clarify the daily operation of an organization. They are requests for information or responses to requests for information. Typically, memos deal with personnel requests, maintenance, and training.

Narcotics or Intoxication Report

Narcotics or intoxication reports are used to document the suspect's condition when under the influence of drugs or alcohol. In opiate influence cases, the report may include a diagram showing the location of puncture wounds.

Supplemental Reports

Supplemental or follow-up reports are used to document the actions of an officer other than the original investigating officer. They are also used to record information discovered after the original report is written.

Traffic Accident Reports

Accident reports document the facts at the scene of a traffic collision. The report may include statements of witnesses, diagrams, and photographs. An arrest may occur at a traffic accident. Depending on department policy, the officer may or may not have to complete additional reports, e.g. crime report and arrest report.

USES AND PURPOSES OF REPORTS

Criminal Investigations

Reports are used to coordinate the officers' activities during an investigation. The investigation may be conducted by uniform officers, or be a complex, follow-up investigation conducted by a specialty investigative unit. Reports are used to compare past and current events to determine modus operandi and identify suspect(s).

Crime reports are generally the source document for filing criminal complaints. They are presented to the prosecuting attorney in their original form. All reports written during the investigation of an event are available to both the prosecution and defense attorneys. Police reports are most closely scrutinized by attorneys at this point in the criminal proceedings.

Newspapers and the Media

Crime reports are available to the press. Depending on state law, case law, and department policy, some portions of the crime report may be deleted. However, the press has the right of access to crime reports.

Reference Material

Reports are permanent records and therefore valuable resource material to the agency and officers. Reports are used to determine liability and are frequently used in civil litigation. They can be used by the officer to refresh his memory at the time of trial.

Statistical Data for Crime Analysis

Sophisticated crime analysis is an important part of law enforcement, and reports are the source document for information. Reports are used to identify trends, locations, and methods of operation.

Documentation

Reports document the actions of officers. Police departments are generally reactive to crime, and reports frequently are the best documentation of an agency's actions. They also provide evidence of responsiveness to community concerns.

Officer Evaluation

Reports are a resource for officer evaluation. Supervisors use reports to measure an officer's abilities. Reports reflect an officer's ability to organize information, and to think logically, as well as his level of education, his intelligence, and training. Writing is disclosure. A report reveals officer's deficient abilities that he may not be aware of or realize he has.

Notes

Statistical Reporting

The Federal Bureau of Investigation supervises the voluntary reporting of crime statistics. Because definitions for various offenses differ from state to state, the FBI has established definitions for crime reporting. Annually the FBI issues a summary of offenses. Most states have statistical reporting requirements for some offenses.

Report Reading Audience

Police reports are read by a wide variety of people. Most officers don't realize the paths their reports follow. Depending on the nature of the event, reports are read by any or all of the following

Administrators - for the department and the city / county / state.

Attorneys - prosecution, defense, civil, and judges

Clerical Staff - the records bureau employees

Insurance Companies - attorneys and parties to claims resulting from an incident

Jurors - during the criminal and civil trials

Media - newspaper, radio, and television reporters

Police Departments - agencies cooperating in investigations

Regulatory agencies - department of motor vehicles, alcohol beverage control, consumer affairs, insurance regulators, etc.

Chapter 2

CHARACTERISTICS OF A GOOD REPORT

There are six basic characteristics to a well-written report. The report must be **accurate**, **clear**, **complete**, **concise**, **factual**, and **objective**. Each of these is equally important to the completion of a well-written report.

ACCURATE

Accurate means in exact conformity to fact. In a police report, the facts are reported correctly and specifically.

CLEAR

Clear means the report is plain or evident to the reader; the meaning is unmistakable. The report leaves no doubt in the reader's mind.

COMPLETE

Reports must have all the necessary parts and include the who, what, when, where, why, and how. Crime reports must include the corpus delicti of the crime.

CONCISE

Concise means to express all the necessary information in as few words as possible. It does not imply leaving out part of the facts in the interest of brevity.

FACTUAL

A fact is something real and presented objectively. Facts are things the officer can prove or disprove. Inference and unsubstantiated opinion are not facts and should not be written in police reports. Officers write inferences when they reach conclusion in their reports, based on premises, rather than facts. Unsubstantiated opinions are usually based on premises; however, sometimes they are based on prejudice and bias.

OBJECTIVE

Objective police reports are not influenced by emotion, personal prejudice, or personal opinion. Officers should record all the facts, remembering there are always two sides to each story.

Chapter 3

BUILDING BLOCKS IN THE REPORT WRITING PROCESS

There are five basic building blocks in the report writing process. They are: (1) Interviewing, (2) Note Taking, (3) Organization and Planning, (4) Writing and Narrative, and (5) Proofreading.

INTERVIEWING

An officer's interview of a victim, witness, or suspect is generally the first block in the report writing process. It is also the beginning of the preliminary investigation.

Frequently, it is the interview and preliminary investigation by the first officer on scene that result in the arrest of the suspect, recovery of property, and clearance of the case.

Before an officer can conduct effective interviews and interrogations, he / she must understand the importance of interpersonal communications.

Interpersonal Communications

Communication is the transfer of ideas resulting in an exchange of information. Communication requires a sender, a receiver, and feedback. The officer is the receiver because he asks questions and then listens. The informant is the sender, because he answers the officer's questions. Feedback is answers, gestures, expressions, and questions.

Types of Interpersonal Communication

Non-verbal

There are three types of non-verbal communication officers use or abuse: gestures, facial expression, and body language.

Gestures should be non-threatening; typically, open hand gestures to encourage the informant to talk.

Facial expressions reveal the officer's true feelings, i.e. boredom, disbelief, or contempt. Officers should master the use of facial expression to convey their intent and prompt the informant to provide more information.

Body language is the overt expression of an officer's feelings and meaning. Body language is easily read by victims, witnesses, and suspects. Officers can use their body language to encourage or discourage an informant. The positive use of body language will improve the officer's ability to gather information.

Verbal

There are five types of verbal communication: one-way, two-way, oral-in person, oral-telephone, and written.

One-way communication is lecture or direction. Officers use one-way communication in high risk situations such as felony car stops or crimes in progress. It is effective in those situations, but not appropriate for interviews and interrogations.

Two-way communication involves the exchange of ideas and information and is the combination of talking and listening.

Oral-in-person communication allows each participant to hear and see the other person. This allows the officer to use his non-verbal communication skills and read the non-verbal communication of the informant.

Oral-telephone is a more restrictive form of communication. The use of non-verbal communication has been eliminated. Frequently, the only contact a citizen has with the police department is by telephone. At the time of the contact, the citizen is judging the entire department on a single telephone conversation. Put yourself in the position of the caller; be professional, polite, courteous, and helpful.

Written communication is the most difficult for officers to master. One reason is the lengthy turn around time between writing the report and getting feedback (return of the report). When an officer writes a report, he discloses something about himself. Usually, the disclosure reveals strengths or weaknesses in his ability to organize information, his education, training, or professional ability.

Three-Step Interview Method

The Three-Step Interview Process is a simple method to conduct interviews. When learning the process, think of routine report calls. Try the Three-Step Method on a simple theft or vandalism report. After you've practiced it, you'll find it can be used to conduct any interview or interrogation.

1. Subject Tells the Story

The officer listens, keeping the subject on track, and giving him verbal and non-verbal clues to keep the story flowing. The officer takes no notes and tries to establish a rapport with the subject. The officer is also checking whether he has jurisdiction, determining what crime, if any, has occurred, and watching for any signs of untruthfulness or discrepancies. At the conclusion of this phase, the officer should know what occurred and what action he must take, and, specifically, the type of report to complete.

2. Subject Retells the Story and the Officer Takes Notes

The officer now has the subject at ease and gathers identifying information from the subject. The officer asks questions and guides the subject through the story a second time. The officer has already determined the type of event and what reports or actions he must take. During this phase, the officer establishes the chronological order and corpus delicti of the crime. He asks questions in the specific order he wants to write the report, thereby organizing his report as he interviews and takes notes.

3. Officer Reads His Notes to the Informant

The officer reviews his notes and reads them back to the informant. This phase allows both the officer and the informant to catch any mistakes or omissions. It also represents the first time the officer writes his report, because in reading his notes out loud, he's actually dictating the report.

NOTE: Use of the Three-Step Interview Method provides credibility for officers testifying in court. If the defense raises the question of discrepancies in an informant's story or between what was said and what was recorded, the Three-Step Method documents the officer's interview.

Interrogation

Interrogations are interviews of suspects in crimes. Officers use the same communications skills for an interrogation as an interview.

The basic difference between an interrogation and an interview is that an interrogation has a plan. Generally during an interrogation, police officers don't ask questions they don't know the answers to. That doesn't mean the answer they get is the answer they expected.

The concept is they have a plan and may even write down specific questions or points they want to ask about during an interrogation. There is nothing in an interrogation to justify coercion or excessive force.

NOTE TAKING

Definition

Notes are brief notations concerning specific events that are recorded while fresh in the officer's mind and used to prepare a report.

Purposes of Notes

Notes are the basis for writing reports. They provide a greater degree of accuracy than memory alone for specific facts, e.g. names, dates of birth, serial numbers, descriptions, etc. When an officer takes neat and accurate notes, he reduces the need to recontact victims and witnesses.

Notes are evidence and subject to the scrutiny of the court.

Defense attorneys attempt to develop impeachable inconsistencies between the officer's notes and his reports.

If officers take neat, accurate, and thorough notes, it adds to their credibility and takes away from the defense efforts to discredit the officer on the witness stand.

Notes provide a permanent reference source for officers. Officers record information about specific calls on their pads. They also record information from roll call or briefing, e.g. information about suspects, cars, property, etc.

Notes

Permanent Notes

Permanent notes are taken onto a spiral pad, or some other similar notebook. It is the officer's responsibility to save the pads. The notes provide a permanent record of the officer's activities. Permanent notes are the recommended method for note taking.

Note Pads

A permanent note taking method requires a note pad the officer can save. The size and design of the pad is at the discretion of the officer. Two types of pads are most commonly used: a pocket pad and a "steno" pad or spiral notebook.

The front cover or first page should include the officer's identification: name, badge number, agency name and / or division or precinct, and dates the pad includes. By putting this information on the cover, the officer can file them in chronological order for easy reference.

Content of Notes

Daily Entries

When an officer begins each shift, he may want to include all or part of the following information:

- Day

- Date

- Shift

- Area or beat

- Partner's name

- Supervisor's name

- Watch commander's name

- Unique weather conditions

- Special assignments

- Briefing information

Some agencies require officers to record information such as the unit number of their police car, mileage, and equipment serial numbers. Officers may want to record this on their pads as well as on their daily activity report (log), in case the log is lost.

Criminal Investigations

Depending on the type of incident and the officer's responsibilities at a crime scene, the officer may be required to record the following:

- Victim statements

- Witness statements

- Suspect statements, description, direction of travel

- Notifications: include time of notification and time of arrival if appropriate of the supervisor, watch commander, investigators, and other agencies

- Evidence: include chain of evidence information - the name of the discoverer, location, time, condition, and disposition.

- Officers' arrival times

- Weather conditions

- Lighting conditions

- Scene conditions

- Victim condition, location, method of transportation if removed, name of ambulance driver, paramedics, etc.

- Modus Operandi information

Non-Criminal Calls

Frequently, officers handle calls requiring reports that are not criminal events. Typically, these are medical aid calls and civil disputes. Officers notes may include the following:

Notes

- Name, address, phone number, and date of birth of persons involved

- Relationship among those involved

- Name of ambulance transporting victim(s)

- Name and address of hospital

- Name of physician and his opinion

- Reason for the dispute

- Officer's actions to resolve situation

- Evidence collected, including chain of evidence

Mechanics of Note Taking

Scratch Outlining

The scratch outline contains a key sentence and supporting points. It is a simple, methodical, and easy to use method for note taking. It's used for short speeches, reports, paragraphs, developing answers for essays, and note taking.

In police report writing, use the scratch outline to organize your information before writing the report. Take notes during the interview using the scratch outline.

Example of a note pad with a scratch outline:

Key Sentence

John Smith was arrested for resisting arrest and assault with a deadly weapon.

Supporting Points

- Off. Kelly asked for ID

- Smith refused

- Smith grabbed ID from Kelly

- Smith tried to run

- Off. O'Brian stopped him

- Smith pointed gun at O'Brian

- Kelly grabbed Smith from behind

- Smith was booked into jail at 0235 hrs.

Remember to leave space between lines; don't crowd everything together. During step three of the interview, you may need to add information. When you begin to organize the information, you may need the space for changes.

Scratch outlines don't have a set format; each one is different. During step two of the interview, the officer guides the informant through the story. He knows what he needs to record on his pad to complete the report. The officer asks question in chronological order. Each question could be a key sentence, depending on the informant's response. Some officers will need to write lengthy notes; others will write brief notes. This is why scratch outlining is so effective; the notes are customized.

In school, writing is taught in a similar method. Teachers use the topic sentence to teach paragraph development. The principle is the same, except police officers have to gather the information from interviews and take notes. In English composition classes, the students create the information.

Tape Recorder

The use of a tape recorder for field note taking is generally discouraged. The exception is specific suspect interviews and/or interrogations.

The problems with tape recording field notes are: equipment malfunction and too much unnecessary information is captured.

If you use a tape recorder for suspect interviews, always include:

- Your name

- Rank

- Department

- Date and time

- Case number and type of case

Notes

Tape recorders may play an important role in obtaining unsolicited suspect statements where no violation of *Miranda* can destroy the use of the statements as evidence, e.g. a recorder left on in a patrol car after suspects have been arrested and prior to *Miranda*.

REMEMBER - There is no substitute for good note taking.

ORGANIZATION AND PLANNING

Reports must be clearly organized. If the narrative skips around and changes from one topic to another, the reader is confused. Officers should organize their reports on their note pads.

During the second step of the interview, the officer begins organizing his report by asking questions in chronological order. In the third step, he reads his notes back to the informant and is actually writing the narrative. It is during these two steps of the interview and note taking process that most of the organization should take place. Once the interview and note taking are complete, the officer can review his notes to make any necessary adjustments.

The planning and organization of a report is closely related to chronological order. Your notes are the road-map to a completed report.

WRITING THE NARRATIVE

After completing a thorough interview or interrogation and taking complete and accurate notes, the next step is to write the narrative. If your agency uses the one-write system, your handwritten report is the source document; that means it is the original. If your agency uses a dictation or tape recorder method, your report is transcribed by a clerk and that document becomes the original.

During Step Three of the interview, you read your notes back to the informant. When you do that, you basically write your report. Now you just need to put it on paper. Review your notes and decide what forms or reports your agency requires to document the event.

Report Dictation

Dictating reports is much easier if you followed the Three-Step Interview and scratch outline note taking methods. The combination of these two methods is called a "dictation tree."

These are the basic rules for dictating reports.

1. First, organize your thoughts by reviewing your notes.

2. Relax for a few minutes after reviewing your notes.

3. When you first begin to dictate:

   - state the type of report (what form to use)

   - state your name and badge number

   - follow the order of the blocks on the form

   - slow your speech slightly

   - speak clearly, spell out names and words that are not easily understood

   - do not loose concentration, don't try to listen for radio calls, etc.

   - do not smoke, drink, chew gum, or eat during dictation

   - if you make a mistake, pause, then tell the operator that you need to make a correction

   - when finished, restate your name and badge number

   - use simple courtesy, "thank you operator"

PROOFREADING

The final building block is one of the most important; proofreading. After you have finished the police report, don't just turn it in. Take a few minutes and proofread. It takes far less time to make a simple correction before you turn in the report, than after it has been reviewed by a supervisor and returned to you.

Check your report for the correct format and that you used the correct form. Take this opportunity to check spelling, grammar, sentence structure, punctuation, and for active voice.

Read the report for specific content; the elements of the crime (corpus delicti), chronological order, and overall appearance. This is your last chance to catch your own mistakes.

Chapter 4

CHRONOLOGICAL ORDER

Generally there are two chronological orders in police reports, (1) the order of the officer's activities and (2), the order of the event.

The exception is an observation or officer initiated event. If an officer observes an event and becomes a participant, his chronological order is the same as the chronological order of the event.

OFFICER'S ORDER OF ACTIVITY

The officer:

- Interviews the victim

- Interviews any witnesses

- Stops and arrests the suspect, if possible

- Accounts for his activity, e.g. books suspect

The report is written in the chronological order of the officer's activities. The facts of the event are written in the order of the event.

ORDER OF THE EVENT

The order of the event is outlined below. The notes are in the order the officer investigated the crime. Each interview contains the facts of the event in the order they occurred.

Example

Victim Jones said -

- 7:30 am went to work
- 5:30 pm came home
- front door open
- TV missing from family room
- called police

Witness Lee said -

- 9:00 am saw man at Jones's house

- carrying TV to car

- able to give description

Officer North -

- saw suspect driving down street

- stopped and arrested him

- interrogated suspect

Suspect said -

- went to house at 9:00 am

- took TV

- walked out front door & drove away

Officer North -

- booked the suspect at county jail

REMINDER: The example is written in scratch outline format. Review the section on note taking as a refresher if you've forgotten the use of the Scratch Outline.

OBSERVATION / OFFICER INITIATED ACTIVITY

When the officer makes an observation arrest, his chronological order is the order of the event.

The officer sees the violation and takes action.

Example

Officer

- sees event-suspect drinking beer in city park

- stops the suspect

- confiscates the beer

- interviews the suspect

Notes

Suspect interview

- admits it is his beer

Officer

- arrests suspect

The officer's observations and actions are part of the report. He documents the event based on his actions, rather than on the actions of someone else.

Chapter 5

FIRST vs. THIRD PERSON STYLE

Police reports are written in either the first or third person style. Both are acceptable. First persons style is the most widely used. Police officers should refer to themselves in police reports as active participants. If you did something, say so.

FIRST PERSON

Examples

- I talked to Mrs. Smith.

- Officer Jones and I searched the building.

The alternative is to use third person. The officer refers to himself as assigned officer, reporting officer, or this officer.

THIRD PERSON

Examples

- This Officer talked to Mrs. Smith.

- Assigned officer and his partner searched the building.

Usually department policy specifies which style you use. If given the choice, use first person. Police reports should be written in an easily understandable style. When we interview a victim, witness, or suspect, we're actively involved.

Chapter 6

CLEAR AND CONCISE WRITING STYLE

A clear, concise report means it does not contain unnecessary information and uses few words as possible to record the necessary facts. The report conveys only one meaning to the reader.

The areas to consider when improving the clarity and conciseness of reports are Active Voice Writing Style, Modifiers, Parallelism, Noun-Pronoun Agreement, and Word Choice.

ACTIVE VOICE WRITING STYLE

Use of the "Active Voice Writing Style" is the easiest way to write clear, concise sentences. Writing in active voice allows the report writing officer to:

- Decrease sentence length by 20%

- Directly answer the question, Who did the action?

- Eliminate punctuation errors

Active Voice enables the writer to avoid weak and awkward sentences. It simplifies the language of the report. The reports are easier to read and less confusing.

The differences between a sentence written in active voice versus passive voice are pace, clarity, and vigor.

Example

Joe hit him. (Active voice)

He was hit by Joe. (Passive voice)

THREE STEPS TO WRITING ACTIVE VOICE SENTENCES

Step One

Locate the ACTION of the sentence.

Step Two

Locate who or what is doing the action. This is the DOER of the sentence. If the DOER is implied and not written in, or it is being acted on by the ACTION, the sentence is weak (passive). If the DOER is written but not located just in front of the verb, the sentence is weak.

Step Three

Put the DOER immediately in front of the ACTION.

Examples

- The sergeant called a squad meeting. (Active voice)

- Detective Peterson found the revolver on the floor. (Active voice)

- A call was received at 1530 hrs. (Passive voice)

Step One -

What's the action? "*was received*"

Step Two -

Who is the DOER? The sentence doesn't have a DOER, so decide who received the call: "*I*"

Step Three -

Put the DOER immediately in front of the ACTION: "*I received the call at 1530 hrs.*"

MODIFIERS

A modifier explains, describes, and / or limits some other word in the sentence and should be placed, in most cases, as close to that word as possible. Modifiers can be single words or phrases.

Adjectives

Adjectives modify nouns and pronouns. They answer the questions which one, what kind, and how many.

Example

>The suspect drove a shiny, red car.
>
>("Shiny and red" are adjectives modifying car.)

Adverbs

Adverbs modify verbs, adjectives, and other adverbs. They answer the questions when, where, how, how much, to what extent.

Example

>The officer closely followed the suspect.
>
>("Closely" is an adverb and modifies followed.)

Prepositional Phrases

Prepositional phrases are words which show relationships between nouns and other words. They can be particularly tricky in technical writing, such as police reports.

Example

>Betty, injured in the accident, will be off work for a month.
>
>("Injured in the accident" is a prepositional phrase modifying Betty.)

Misplaced Modifiers

Misplaced modifiers, often quite humorous, can be very embarrassing and give an inaccurate account of the events in a report.

Examples

>He has only a face that a mother could love. (*incorrect*)
>
>He has a face that only a mother could love. (*correct*)

Dangling Modifiers

A modifier should have a word in the same sentence to which it is clearly and logically related.

Examples

> In order to pass the sergeant's test, it is necessary for me to study regularly. (*incorrec*t)

> In order to pass the sergeant's test, I must study regularly. *(correct)*

Squinting Modifiers

A squinting modifier looks in two directions at once.

Examples

> Anyone who reads the log frequently will notice that many officers are now handling more calls.

> "Frequently" is between two verbs, "reads" and "will notice". It should be rewritten, depending on the writer's intent.

> Anyone who frequently reads...

> or

> Anyone who reads the log will notice frequently...

Parallelism

Parallel ideas should be expressed in parallel structure.

Example

Incorrect

> John was a *miser*, a *bachelor*, and *egotistical*.
>   (noun)   (noun)   (adjective)

Correct

> John was a *miser*, a *bachelor*, and an *egotist*.
>   (noun) (noun)   (noun)

AGREEMENT

Pronouns

Pronouns are words which take the place of nouns. All pronouns must agree with their antecedents in person, number, and gender. An antecedent is the noun that usually appears before the pronoun. The pronoun takes the place of the antecedent. Pronouns refer to something clearly visible in sentence. The pronouns "it" and "they" must refer to specific nouns.

Example

Incorrect

If the police dog won't eat its food, try covering it with warm gravy.

Correct

If the police dog won't eat his food, try covering the food with warm gravy.

Subject-Verb

A verb (ACTION) of a sentence must agree with its subject (DOER) in number. Singular subjects require singular verbs and plural subjects require plural verbs.

Examples

The *box* of food *has been found.*
  (subject)   (verb) both singular

Most of the boxes of food *have been found.*
(subject)   (verb) both plural

WORD CHOICE

Deadwood Words

Writing police reports in active voice reduces sentence length by 20%. Some officers continue writing lengthy sentences by adding unnecessary words. These words and phrases are fancy, formal, or grand expressions which usually serve no purpose. Officers' reports should use common, everyday words that are understood by everyone, especially judges and jurors.

Officers don't appear to be more intelligent by using lengthy prepositional phrases and multi-syllable words. Most sentences in police reports should be 12-15 words long.

300 Deadwood Words

Instead of...	Try...
abeyance	delayed or held up
accomplish, execute, perform	do
accordingly	therefore, so, that is why
accumulate	gather
acquaint	tell
acquire, secure	get
additional	added
ad infinitum	endlessly
adverse	poor, bad
advise	write, inform, tell
afford an opportunity	allow, permit, let
aforementioned, aforesaid	these
aggregate	total
a good deal	much
a great deal of the time	often
a limited quantity of	few
all of	all
along the lines	like, the same way
alteration, revision	change
altercation	fight
ameliorate	improve
analyzation	analysis
answer in the affirmative	say yes
anticipate	foresee
apparent	clear
appears that	clear
appended	added
applicable	apply to
are desirous of	want
are in receipt of	have received
as a matter of fact	in fact
ascertain	discover, find out
as per	according to

Notes

Instead of...	Try...
assistance	aid help
assuming that	if
at a later date	later
at an early date	soon
at such time	when
at the present time	now
attached you will find	attached is
attribute	due
balance of	remainder, rest
basis, based on,	on, by, after, for, because
on the basis of	on, by, after, for, because
be in position to	can
beneficial aspects of	benefits
broken down into	divided into
bulk of	most
by means of	by, with
check into	check
classifications	classes
close proximity	near, or just "close"
cognizance	knowledge
cognizant of	know
commence	start
commitment	promise
compensate, compensation	pay,
concur	agree
consensus of opinion	consensus
consequently	so
consider favorably	approved
considerable	much, serious, grave
construct	build
contacted	spoke to, visited,
contingent upon receipt of	when we receive
continuous basis	continually
contribute	give
deleterious, detrimental	harmful
demonstrate	show
despite the fact that	although
direct effort toward	try
due in large measure to	due largely
due to the fact that	because
during the time that	while
during the course of	during
effect a reduction of	reduce
employ	use
encounter	meet
endeavor	try
equivalent	equal
excessive amount	too much
exit	leave

Instead of...	Try...
expense	cost
expedite	hasten, hurry, speed
explicit	plain
facilitate	make easy, simplify
feasible	possible
feels	believes, thinks,
finalize	finish, end
following	after
forthcoming	coming
for the reason that	because, since
for the purpose of	for, to
found to be	are
forward, furnish, transmit	send
frequently	often
furthermore	also, in addition
gainfully employed	working, employed
give consideration to	consider
give instruction to	instruct
have a need for	need
henceforth, hereafter	from now on, in the future
herein	here
hereinafter	after this
hereinbefore	until now
heretofore	up to now, until now
herewith	with this now
imminent	near (in time)
implement, implementation	carry out, set up, enforce,
in advance of, prior to	before
in accordance with	with, by, as, under
in a most careful manner	carefully
in a number of cases	some, many
in a timely manner	promptly
in connection with	with
in the amount of	for
inasmuch as	because
indebtedness	debt
indicate, state	show, tell, said, noted,
initial	first
initiate	begin, start
in lieu of	instead of
in many cases	many
in order that	so
in order to	to
inquired into, inquired as to	studied, examined, asked about
in regard to	concerning
in relation to	about
in spite of the fact that	although
institute	start, begin
in the affirmative	yes, agreed

Notes

Notes

Instead of...	Try...
in the course / case of	in, at, or, during, while
in the event of / that	if
in the magnitude of	about
in the majority of cases	usually
in the matter of	in, about
in the very near future	soon
in the time of	during
in the vicinity of	near
in this day and age	today
in view of the fact	since, because
in large measure	largely
is as follows	follows
it is our opinion	we feel, believe
it is our understanding that	we understand
it is my understanding that	I understand
justification for	reason for
kindly arrange to send	please send
locality	place
locate	find, put
likewise	and also
maintenance	upkeep
make a decision	decide
make a determination	determine
make application for	apply
make inquiry regarding	ask
modification	change
nevertheless	but, however
nonavailability of	unavailable
notwithstanding	despite, in spite of
numerous	many
objective	aim
obligate	bind
obligation	debt
observed	saw
obtain	get
occasion	cause
on a few occasions	occasionally
on behalf of	for
on the basis of	by, from, because
on the grounds that	because
on the occasion of	when
on the part of	for, among
on the subject of	about
optimum	the most for the least
orientated	oriented
outside of	outside
owing to the fact that	because

Instead of...	Try...	Notes
participate	take part	
per diem, per annum	per day, a year	
pertain	about on	
peruse	read	
place emphasis on	emphasize	
possess	have	
preventative	preventive	
prior to	before	
proceed	go	
procure	get	
provided, providing	if	
regarding	about	
realize a savings of	save	
reimburse	pay	
related with, relates to, relating to, relative to	on, about	
render aid or assistance	help	
reported	said, told	
resided	lived	
residence	house, apartment,	
responded	answered, said	
sibling	brother, sister	
subject matter	subject, topic	
submit	send, give,	
subsequently, subsequent to	later, afterward, then, next	
sufficient	enough	
summarization	summary	
sustained	received	
take action	act	
terminate, terminated	end, ended, stopped, ending	
the question as to whether	whether	
the reason is due to	because	
thereafter	after that, then	
therein	there, in it	
thereof	of it	
thereupon	then	
this is a subject that	this subject	
transmit	send	
transported	took, drove	
under date of	on	
under the circumstances	because	
until such time as	until	
utilization, utilize	use	
vehicle	car, truck,	
visualize	see, think of, imagine	

Notes

Instead of...	Try...
whereby	by which, so that
wherein	in which, where, when
whether or not	whether
wish to advise, wish to state	(avoid, do not use)
with regard to	about, regarding, concerning
with reference to	about, regarding, concerning
with respect to	about, regarding, concerning
with the result that	so that
without further delay	immediately, soon, quickly
would seem, would appear	seem / appear (try to avoid these)

Word Meanings

Use simple everyday words. Avoid using slang or jargon unless you are quoting someone.

Definitions

- Slang - inappropriate street language

- Jargon - the specialized language of a profession. Avoid using undefined penal codes & radio codes.

Examples of police jargon

Instead of...	*Use...*
contact	called, talked to
stated	said
observed	saw
exit, exited	leave, left
negative results	empty, couldn't find
it should be noted that	furthermore

Specific examples of poor or incorrect word meanings

already	by this or a specified time
all ready	all things are ready
among	three or more in a group
between	in a position between two; or interval separating
appear to	to come into view, become visible
seems to	to give the impression of being
as	to the same extent or degree, equally
when	at what time
canvas	a heavy, coarse fabric
canvass	to examine thoroughly; to solicit
counsel	consultation or a lawyer
council	a body of people elected by voters
effect	result, the way something acts on an object
affect	to have an influence on, influence, impress
elude	to evade or escape
allude	to make an indirect reference to
past	no longer current
passed	to move on ahead, proceed
principle	a basic truth, law
principal	foremost in rank or worth
stationary	not moving, not capable of being moved
stationery	writing paper
trustee	a person or agent in a position of trust
trusty	an inmate worker in prison or jail
upon	on, to put on top of
when	at what time

Chapter 7

RULES OF GRAMMAR, PUNCTUATION, & MECHANICS

GRAMMAR

Adjectives

An adjective modifies (describes, limits, makes more exact) a noun or pronoun. Adjectives appear close to the words they modify.

Examples

> The male suspect
>
> The injured victim

Adverbs

An adverb modifies or describes a verb, an adjective, or another adverb.

Examples

> The suspect ran quickly. (Modifies a verb)
>
> The very tall suspect.(Modifies an adjective)
>
> The suspect ran very quickly. (Modifies adverb)

Comma Splice

A comma splice is the result of using a comma to separate two sentences. The correct punctuation is a period.

Incorrect

> The officer chased the suspect for three blocks, he arrested him for robbery.

Correct

> The officer chased the suspect for three blocks. He arrested him for robbery.

Run-on Sentence

A run-on sentence results from completely omitting punctuation between two or more sentences.

Incorrect

> When I stopped the suspect he tried to hit me in the face he swung and missed.

Correct

> When I stopped the suspect, he tried to hit me in the face, but he swung and missed.

Sentence Fragments

A sentence fragment is group of words, punctuated as a sentence, that does not express a complete thought. It does not contain a main clause.

Incorrect

> I searched the house. Knowing I'd find him there.

Correct

> I searched the house, knowing I'd find him there.

PUNCTUATION

Apostrophe [']

Apostrophes are used to form contractions and possessives.

Contractions shorten words without changing the meaning. It is acceptable in police reports to use contractions. The apostrophe is used to indicate the omission of letters in words or numbers in a date.

Examples

- Couldn't (means could not)

- Shouldn't (means should not)

- Don't (means do not)

- Class of '88

Possessives show ownership. The rules to form a possessive are:

Notes

Singular Possessive - Add ('s) to all nouns, whether they end in "s" or not.

Examples

Brad's gun...

Jones's gun...

Plural Possessive - either:

Add (') to plural nouns ending in "s"

Example

Officers' guns...

or

Add ('s) to plural nouns not ending in "s"

Example

Women's guns...

Colon [:]

A colon is used to introduce statements, lists, and explanations. It is also used in hours and ratios.

Examples

The Chief began his briefing with these words: "You are the finest officers in the country."

The evidence technician collected the following: the gun, a knife, a blouse, and a shoe.

The rules and regulations serve two purposes: they protect the department and protect the officer.

The time is 2:30 a.m.

The officer to population ratio is 1:1000.

Semi-Colon [;]

A semi-colon is used between independent clauses not joined by a coordinating conjunction (and, or, nor, for, but, yet, so).

Example

The Chief can't tell us today; he hopes to tell us Friday.

After each clause in a series of three or more independent clauses when they are long

Example

> The radio was quiet; the motor officers were gone; the detective left; and the officer was alone.

Before conjunctive adverbs such as therefore, however, nevertheless, connecting two independent clauses.

Example

> The department is expanding its station; therefore, some offices may be moved.

Between elements in a list when there are commas in the elements.

Example

> The chiefs of the three departments are Davis, San Antonio; Ramos, Tucson; and Allen, Miami.

Comma [,]

Commas are used to separate or set apart elements within a sentence.

Separates *and* or *or* from the final item in a series of three or more.

Example

> The radio, television set, and stereo were arranged on one shelf.

Sets off the year from the month in full dates.

Example

> The City Council appointed the new Chief on May 1, 1988.

Sets off short quotations and sayings.

Example

> The Chief said, "Keep up the good work."

Sets off a nonrestrictive clause or phrase (one that if eliminated would not change the meaning of the sentence).

Example

> The thief, who entered through the window, went straight to the safe.

Sets off words or phrases in apposition (explanatory equivalent) to a noun or noun phrase.

Example

> Jones, the homicide detective, was a motorcycle officer.

Sets off transitional words and short expressions that require a pause in reading or speaking.

Example

> Indeed, the sight of the body gave me quite a jolt.

Sets off words used to introduce a sentence.

Example

> No, I haven't seen her.

Sets off city and state in geographic names.

Example

> Boston, Massachusetts, is the largest city in New England.

Sets off any sentence elements that might be misunderstood if the comma were not used.

Example

> To Mary, Anne was just a nuisance.

Dash [-]

Use a dash to summarize statements, repeat elements, changes in thought, omit letters, and between dates.

Before a summarizing statement beginning with words such as "these" or "all".

Example

> Officers, detectives and sergeants - these officers attended the meeting.

To emphasize repeated expressions.

Example

> He is the suspect - the suspect the police want.

To indicate an abrupt change in thought.

Example

> The first step is - no, come to think of it, that's not the first step.

To indicate missing letters in confidential correspondence.

Example

> This message is for Mr. B-.

In place of *to* and *between* in dates and numbers.

Examples

> He was an officer, 1980-81.
>
> Read pages 25-60.

Exclamation Point [!]

Use an exclamation point to give emphasis to a word, phrase or sentence. Be careful in police reports to only use exclamation points when quoting someone. Officers can't add their own emphasis to points in a police report.

Example

> Drop the gun!

Parenthesis [( )]

Use parenthesis around explanatory, non-essential material within a sentence.

Example

> Officer Ticket (what an appropriate name) works traffic.

To enclose references, directions, and sources of information.

Example

> The crime rate has dropped 5% (FBI).

Around numbers or letters indicating listings or divisions within a sentence.

Example

> He gave three field sobriety tests: (1) finger dexterity, (2) spelling, (3) balance.

To enclose a translation of a phrase.

Notes

Example

The suspect said he'd been to the joint (prison).

Around figures repeated to insure accuracy.

Example

The loss was eighty dollars ($80).

Period [.]

Periods are used at the end of a sentence.

Example

The officer arrested the suspect.

Used with an abbreviation and initials.

Example

Mr. John Brown or Lt. B. L. White or Dr. Small, M.D.

Question Mark [?]

Question marks are used after a direct question.

Example

How many were arrested?

After a short direct question following a statement.

Example

You will arrest him, won't you?

MECHANICS

Capitalization

Use capital letters for:

The first word of a sentence.

Example

He is the new recruit.

The first word of a direct quotation.

Example

      The sergeant said, "He is the new recruit."

The names of people, organizations and their members.

Examples

      William Jones

      The Salinas Police Department

      Officer Garcia

The names of places and geographic areas.

Examples

      San Francisco

      West Coast

      the South, West, North, East

      NOTE - Do not capitalize direction (go south 2 blocks).

The names of rivers, lakes, mountains, etc.

Example

      Los Angeles River

The names of ships, airplanes, and space vehicles.

Examples

      U.S.S. Enterprise

      Apollo II

The names of nationalities, races, tribes, and languages.

Examples

      Spanish

      Mexican

      Caucasian

Words indicating family relationships.

Example

      Aunt Mary

Titles when they proceed names.

Notes

Examples

> Chief John Frank
>
> Lt. Harry McClure

Titles of books and publications.

Example

> The latest edition of Newsweek magazine.

Days, months, and holidays.

Example

> Sunday, December 25th is Christmas.

Courts

Example

> The Superior Court of the State of California

Hyphens [-]

Use hyphens to link words and parts of words.

Example

> pro-police

Show word division when one part of a word is on one line and the rest of it is on another line; remember to divide words at syllables.

Example

> The detective read the sus-
> pect the *Miranda* wavier.

Link numbers (from twenty-one to ninety-nine) and fractions.

Examples

> sixty-two
>
> seven-eights

Numbers

Spell out a number when at the beginning of a sentence

Example

> Ten officers went to the call.

Ages - Use figures only when age is stated in years, months, and days. Write out the age otherwise.

Examples

The baby is 2 years 4 months 10 days old.

The department is one hundred years old.

Use figures for decimals and percentages, unless it is the beginning of the sentence.

Examples

88.5 per cent

Eighty-five per cent of the officers passed.

Use figures and commas to show numbers of four or more digits.

Example

32,987

Use figures for measurements and capacities.

Examples

12 feet

100 lbs.

62 degrees

15 gals.

Spell out military groups or units.

Example

Eighty-Second Airborne

Use figures for definite sums of money.

Example

$569.57

Spell out indefinite sums of money.

Example

The value was about one hundred dollars.

Notes

Quotation Marks [" "]

Use quotation marks to enclose a direct quotation. Do not use them for an indirect quotation.

Examples

> The suspect said, "Gimme the money."

> The witness said the suspect asked for the money.

To enclose unfamiliar words, slang, or jargon.

Example

> Ballard said Smith was an "oddball."

To indicate the names of titles of publications (other than magazines, newspapers, and books), articles, stories, poems, musical pieces, works of art, and plays.

Example

> "The Star Spangled Banner"

Around a defined word or phrase.

Example

> "Unit" or "cruiser" means a police car.

Underlining

Use underlining for the titles of books, magazines, newspapers, pamphlets, movies, and TV programs.

Examples

> Fatal Command (book)

> Adam 12 (TV program)

Chapter 8

PARAGRAPHING

Definition: A paragraph is a group of sentences which tell about one topic. The topic sentence tells what the sentences in the paragraph are about. Usually it is the first sentence in the paragraph. Paragraphing is a method of alerting the reader to a shift of focus in the report.

Review the section on note taking and use of the Scratch Outline format. Scratch outlines have "key sentences." Key sentences are generally "topic sentences" in paragraphing.

STEPS IN WRITING A PARAGRAPH

First

Your notes provide the key or topic sentence and the outline for the paragraphs. Check for completeness and rearrange if necessary.

Second

Write the paragraph in active voice style, using 12-15 word sentences.

Paragraphs in police reports generally have 5-7 sentences or approximately 100 words. However, it is acceptable in police reports to write one or two sentence paragraphs.

One or two sentence paragraphs are used to mark a transition in reports, from one topic or section to another: typically, going from the interview of the victim to the interview of a witness.

Indent the beginning of each paragraph or skip one or two lines between paragraphs.

Unity

- Preserve the unity of the paragraph.

- A paragraph should develop a single topic, the key sentence. Every sentence in the paragraph should contribute to the development of the single idea.

Coherence

- Compose the paragraph so it reads coherently.

- Coherence makes it easy for the reader to follow the facts and events. It reflects clear thinking by the report writer. A clearly stated chronological order of events makes the paragraph and, therefore, the report coherent.

Development

Paragraphs should be adequately developed. Consider the central idea. Present examples or specific quotes. Include relevant facts, details, or evidence. Explore and explain the causes of an event or the motives of the suspect. The result may be an explanation of how the event occurred. Finally,describe the scene, injuries, or other pertinent information.

Suggestions

- Repeat key sentences from paragraph to paragraph.

- Use pronouns in place of key nouns.

- Use "pointing words," e.g. this, that, those, these

- Use "thought-connecting words," such as: however, moreover, also, therefore, thus, indeed, then.

- Arrange sentences in chronological order.

Third

Proofread your work. If necessary, correct mistakes and rewrite the paragraph or report.

Chapter 9

REPORT EDITING

There are ten basic tips to better report writing.

USE ADJECTIVES

Use adjectives to modify nouns or pronouns and answer the questions which one, what kind, and how many. By changing nouns and verbs to adjectives, you can write more concise sentences. One way to change a noun to an adjective is to add "Y."

Example

> The witness identified the suspect's car because it had mud on it. (confusing)

Corrected

> The witness identified the suspect's car because it was muddy. (clear)

RELATED WORDS

Keep related words near each other in sentences. Writing in active voice helps. When related words are separated, a sentence can be confusing.

Example

> The suspect's vehicle, which was found, was a Ford. (confusing)

Corrected

> The police found the suspect's Ford. (clear)

ELIMINATE PHRASES

Try to use single words: "when" or "while".

Example

> As soon as I arrived I identified the suspect.

Corrected

> When I arrived, I identified the suspect.

USE CONCISE WORDS

Try to use the most concise form of a word.

Example

The suspect was dressed in a shabby manner.

Corrected

The suspect was shabbily dressed. (correct)

ELIMINATE USELESS PHRASES OR SAYINGS

Eliminate useless phrases or sayings such as "of a" and "such as".

Example

The officer was of such an opinion, that he thought the suspect was drunk.

Corrected

The officer thought the suspect was drunk.

ELIMINATE "TIVE" AND "TION"

Try to eliminate words ending in "tive" and "tion".

Example

The narcotics officer conducted an examination of the suspect.

Corrected

The narcotics officer examined the suspect.

USE PREFIXES AND SUFFIXES

A prefix is added to the beginning of a word, and a suffix is added to the end of a word. Caution: make sure the word you've created exists; "uncola" is only found in commercials, not dictionaries.

Examples

Officer Jones is sometimes not a happy person.

The suspect is ready to be booked.

Corrected

Sometimes Officer Jones is unhappy.

The suspect is ready for booking.

ELIMINATE "THAT"

"That" can usually be eliminated and not change the meaning of the sentence.

Example

He told me that he was ready for the interview.

Corrected

He told me he was ready for the interview.

ELIMINATE "THEN"

In most sentences you can eliminate the word "then" and not change the meaning of the sentence.

Example

I then went next door to interview the witness.

Corrected

I went next door to interview the witness.

ELIMINATE "WHICH IS" AND "WHO IS"

Try to eliminate phrases like "which is" and "who is".

Example

The evidence, which is listed above, was photographed.

Corrected

The technician photographed the evidence.

Chapter 10

REPORT FORMATS & STYLES

There are two basic formats used to write police reports: narrative and category. Narrative style is the most widely used. Category style is more structured and the format is determined by agency policy. Because it is determined by agency policy, category style reports vary widely from police department to police department.

NARRATIVE STYLE

When writing in narrative style, remember chronological order. In his report, the officer retells the story in the order he discovered the information; his order of activity. Each of the interviews reveals the facts in the order they occurred.

Narrative reports look like a report for school or the text from a book. The officer writes complete sentences and develops paragraphs.

Depending on department policy, you may or may not begin a narrative report with the source of your call. Typically, police departments require a sentence giving the date, time, and the location of the interview. This information generally is already on the crime report. It is recommended you eliminate the useless repetition of this information, unless it has some significance to the event (some agencies may use an "introductory" paragraph. An example is included).

Example

At 1230 hrs. I was dispatched to a residential burglary report and interviewed victim Collins at his home.

Victim Collins told me he locked all of his windows and doors and left for work 0730 hrs. At 1200 hrs. he received a phone call from his neighbor Harding. Harding told Collins there was someone outside of Collins's house.

Collins left work and got home at 1215 hrs. His front door was open and his house had been ransacked. Collins went into the house and discovered his TV was missing from the family room. He was also missing $400 cash in an envelope from the dresser in his master bedroom.

Collins said the sliding glass door in the bedroom was pried open. On the patio outside the door, he found a screwdriver that wasn't his.

Harding told me he was mowing his front lawn at approximately 1130 hrs. and saw a suspicious car park in front of Collins's house. Harding said the suspect got out of the car and walked up to Collins's house. The suspect rang the doorbell and, when no one answered, walked around to the backyard.

Harding went inside his house and called Collins. When he came back outside, the suspect and car were gone.

I gave Collins a victim information card with the case number. I notified Jones in the Identification Bureau to send a technician. When I left the scene I checked the neighborhood for witnesses. No one was home at 328, 338, 329, 339, and 349 Oak Street.

CATEGORY

Category format is more structured than narrative format. Police departments' report writing policies dictate the types of categories in the report. Common categories are source of activity, victim statements, officer's observations, officer's activities, scene, and conclusions.

Each category develops a separate part of the report. The officer writes the category title, then begins his report in narrative style under the title. Category style can be cumbersome and inconvenient.

Example

SOURCE

I was dispatched to a burglary report at 333 Oak St. I met victim Collins there at 1230 hrs.

OFFICER'S OBSERVATIONS

When I arrived, Collins was waiting in the front yard. The door to his house was open. I went inside and saw the house had been ransacked.

Notes

VICTIM'S STATEMENTS

Victim Collins told me he locked all of his windows and doors and left for work at 0730 hrs. At 1200 hrs. he received a phone call from his neighbor Harding. Harding told Collins there was someone outside Collins's house.

Collins left work and got home at 1215 hrs. His front door was open and his house had been ransacked. Collins went into the house and discovered his TV was missing from the family room. He was also missing $400 cash in an envelope from the dresser in his master bedroom.

Collins said the sliding glass door in the bedroom was pried open. On the patio outside the door, he found a screwdriver that wasn't his.

WITNESS STATEMENTS

Harding told me he was mowing his front lawn at approximately 1130 hrs. and saw a suspicious car park in front of Collins's house. The suspect got out of the car and walked up to Collins's house. The suspect rang the doorbell and, when no one answered, walked around to the back yard.

Harding went inside his house and called Collins. When he came back outside, the suspect and car were gone.

OFFICER'S ACTIONS

I gave Collins a victim information card with the case number. I notified Jones in the Identification Bureau to send a technician. When I left the scene I checked the neighborhood for witnesses. No one was home at 328, 338, 329, 339, and 349 Oak Street.

SPECIAL PARAGRAPHS

Special paragraphs are used in police reports to point out important information. Generally, the information is technical and easier to understand in a separate paragraph.

Loss

Value - The value of stolen property should be the "fair market value." Fair market value is defined as the value of the property for a quick sale. It is not the replacement value of the property. If there is no value to the property taken, use the word "nil" in place of value.

Examples of "nil" value:

- Credit cards

- Drivers' licenses

- License plates

- Miscellaneous papers

No Real Value - There is no real value for used clothing, with the exception of furs. Value used clothing at garage sale prices.

Commercial Thefts - The store's cost of stolen items is listed, not the retail price tag value.

The field officer should make every effort to determine the value of the property. If for some reason he cannot, notify the field supervisor or check the department report writing manual.

Negotiable Instruments - Negotiable instruments, such as bonds payable to bearer, cashiers checks, money orders, etc. are valued at the current market price at the time of theft.

Non-negotiable Instruments - No value (NIL) should be recorded for non-negotiable instruments, such as checks and securities. The face amount should be included in the description of the loss.

Notes

Description

The loss or property-taken paragraph should contain a complete description of the stolen items. Most departments have report forms with headings or special report forms to record lost or stolen property. Headings include the following:

- Brand name

- Model Name and / or Number

- Serial Numbers

- Description

- Owner Inscribed Numbers

- Miscellaneous Description

Be as detailed as possible: include dimensions, colors, types of materials, and sizes.

Jewelry

In the case of jewelry, ask for photographs or appraisals. If the victim doesn't have either of those, you may want to ask him / her to draw a picture of the piece. The more detailed the description, the better chance of recovery.

Usually each item of jewelry is considered one piece. Exceptions are earrings and matching bracelets.

- Type of Metal (color and kinds, e.g. white or yellow gold, silver)

- Type of Stone(s) (number, kind, color, and size)

- Type of Mounting (filigree, plain, engraved, etc.)

- Type of Setting (basket, Tiffany, box, etc.)

- Type of Inscription (dates, initials, jeweler's marks)

- Style of Jewelry (Indian, antique, or modern)

Example

(1) Man's Wristwatch, B / N Timex, with a round face and sweep second hand, roman numerals, white face and silver color case, approx. 3 yrs. old, engraved on the back, "To Bob"

VALUE: $20.00

Clothing and Furs

Describe the clothing article by including the size, color, maker's label, and kinds of material.

Example

(1) Pair Men's Levi "501" jeans, size 32" x 31", faded, with a hole in the right hip pocket.

VALUE: $3.00

Currency

U.S. currency should be listed first. If some serial numbers are known, list those first and the unknown serial number bill second. Include the following

- Number of bills by denomination e.g. (5) $20 bills

- Serial numbers, if known

- Condition of bills

- Wrappers or envelopes containing the money
Foreign currency is recorded the same as U.S. currency, using the appropriate denominations for the issuing country. Some departments will list the value as "NIL" because field officers aren't expected to know the exchange rates (check department policy).

Example

U.S. Currency: (3) $100 bills, serial #1288394, 1288395, 1288396	$300.00
(3) $20 bills, unknown serial numbers	$60.00

Coins

U.S. and foreign coins are recorded the same as currency.

Example

U.S. Coins: (100) pennies in a paper coin roll $ 1.00

Negotiable or Non-negotiable Instruments

Obtain as much identifying information as possible. Include bank name and branch, or the corporation issuing the bonds or money order.

- Account number

- Amount and value

- Dates

- Names of payee or holder

- Check number(s)

- Color or design of checks

Example

(1) Blank Personal Check from City Bank, Main St. Branch, Acc't. #306-498, Mr. John Lostit, check #212

VALUE: nil

Firearms

Firearms are weapons that fire a projectile by the force of an explosion or the expelling of gas or air. Include all handguns, rifles, shotguns, and other items commonly referred to as a firearm (.177 cal. and up).

- Description should include the following

- Manufacturer

- Model and serial number

- Caliber or gauge

- Barrel length

Other descriptors -

- Automatic
- Bolt action
- Carbine
- Derringer
- Double-barrel
- Gas or air

- Semi-automatic
- Slide or pump action
- Revolver
- Black powder
- Over-under
- Flint-lock

Miscellaneous items include grips, handles, or finishes. If holsters are also taken, list those separately.

Example

(1) Smith & Wesson Mod. 19, Combat Masterpiece, 4" barrel, blue steel finish, with dark wood grips, serial #K192765

VALUE: $285.00

Vehicle Thefts

Car thefts are usually reported on special forms. Generally the following is required

- Year - if unknown estimate ("81-84")
- Make - the manufacture's trade name
- Body Type - 2 door, Limousine, 4 door, Station Wagon, Convertible, Motor Home, Hatchback, Hearse, Bus, 3 door, Utility Vehicle, Ambulance
- Model
- Color
- Vehicle Identification Number (VIN)
- License number and state
- Color of plates
- Special marks
- Body damage
- Window tinting
- Wheels / rims
- Bumper stickers
- Tires
- Antennas - car phones

EVIDENCE

Evidence collected at a crime scene should be listed in a separate paragraph or a special evidence report. If a special report form is used, refer to it in the initial crime report.

At a major crime, it is suggested officers attach copies of the evidence tags or evidence reports to their original crime report.

When a field officer calls for another officer or technician to perform the forensic investigation, list that fact in the evidence paragraph on the crime report.

Chain of Evidence

When evidence is collected at a crime scene, it is essential for the officers to document the chain of evidence.

- Who collected the evidence.

- When did they do it.

- Where did they collect it from.

- What did they do with it.

The description of the evidence is listed in the evidence paragraph. The facts explaining the chain of evidence are listed in the narrative.

Description of Evidence

List evidence in numerical order, counting each item as one in a group of several other items; e.g. 1 / 3 means one of three items or the first item out of a total of three items.

Include

- Quantity

- Article

- Brand

- Model

- Serial Number

- Color

- Other Description

In some states or for some courts, the officer may have to describe the substance before he can conclude what it is; e.g. a green leafy substance (means marijuana). In narcotic cases, officers may have to perform presumptive tests and include the result in the evidence description.

Examples

1 /4 (1) standard head screwdriver, 6" long with a yellow plastic handle

2 /4 (1) pair of tennis shoes

3 /4 (6) Open 12 oz. bottles of Suds beer, cold to the touch and half full of a light brown carbonated liquid that smelled like beer.

 4 /4 (1 gr.) Cocaine (determined by chemical test)

DAMAGE

Damage paragraphs are frequently used in vandalism reports. The officer summarizes the damage at the beginning of the report.

Example

> Damage: The rear window of the victim's '87 Ford was shattered.

INJURIES

Injury paragraphs are frequently used in assault reports to document and quickly summarize the victim's injuries.

Example

> Injuries: The victim required 3 stitches to close a 1 / 2" cut on his / her chin.

PROPERTY RECOVERED

When property is recovered, it is listed on either a special property report or in a special paragraph. The information is the same as in a Loss Paragraph (see above).

SOLVABILITY FACTORS

There are certain factors that can predict the likelihood of solving a crime, i.e. solvability factors. Depending on agency policy, these factors may be printed on the crime report, or the officer may be required to include them in a special paragraph.

Examples

- Was there a witness to the crime?

- Was the suspect arrested?

- Is a suspect named?

- Can a suspect be located?

- Can a suspect be described?

- Can a suspect be identified?

- Can a suspect vehicle be identified?

- Is there an unusual MO?

- Is there significant physical evidence present? Did forensics personnel (CSI or ID) respond?

- Is there major injury / sex crime involved?

- Is there good possibility of solution?

- Is stolen property traceable / identifiable?

- Are serial numbers of stolen property available?

- Were serial numbers entered into the computer?

Chapter 11

CHECKLIST FOR CRIME REPORT NARRATIVES

PROBABLE CAUSE - STOP, DETENTION, ARREST

Officers must articulate their probable cause for stop, detention, and arrest. Use specific terms and words.

Include your observations of suspicious activity. Be thorough and complete. You may need to include your prior training, experience, or arrests / calls to establish what is suspicious to, "a reasonable person".

Include

- Radio broadcasts

- Citizen information

- Special bulletins

- Prior reports

- Prior arrests

Examples

Probable Cause to Stop

I saw suspect Brown driving N / B in the 3400 block of Main St. He failed to stop for the stop sign at Maple St., a violation of Vehicle Code Sec. 22450.

Probable Cause to Detain

I stopped Brown in the 3500 block of Main Street.

Probable Cause to Arrest

I wrote Brown a ticket for failing to stop at the stop sign.

PROBABLE CAUSE - SEARCH AND SEIZURE

When evidence is seized without a warrant, the officer must articulate his probable cause for the search and seizure. Include all pertinent information such as:

- Consent search

- Search incident to a lawful arrest

- Plain view (the eye can commit no trespass)

- Exigent circumstances

- Crime in progress

Example

> I walked up to the driver's side door of Brown's car. Brown rolled down the window and handed me his driver's license. When I looked inside the window, I saw a gun on the seat next to Brown.

CORPUS DELICTI - ELEMENTS OF THE CRIME

The elements of the crime must be specifically stated in the narrative. If you aren't sure of the elements, look in the penal code. Some agencies require a "synopsis" paragraph which includes the corpus delicti.

Examples

> Synopsis: Unknown suspect entered the locked house with the intent to steal the television.

or

> The suspect pried open the sliding glass door and went into the house. He took the TV from the living room.

PENALTY ENHANCING CIRCUMSTANCES

Depending on state law, there may be special circumstances that enhance the penalty for crimes. The officer must include those circumstances in his report.

Examples

- Use of a gun

- Use of a deadly weapon

- Commission of a crime during darkness

- Commission of a crime against a public official

- Inflicting great bodily harm or injury

- Prior arrests and convictions for the same crime

- Under the influence of alcohol or drugs

MIRANDA

Because of changing case law, the requirements change for the *Miranda* admonishment and waiver. Some agencies have *Miranda* advisement report forms.

In your report, you must include the following:

- Source for reading the warning (printed card)

- The exact questions you asked about understanding and waiving their rights

- The suspect's exact response, in quotation marks

MODUS OPERANDI

Factors determining Modus Operandi (M.O.)

Time of Day

Notes

Example

    early morning, darkness, etc.

Type of Victim

Example

    elderly, young

Type of Premises or Location

Example

    single family residence in a residential neighborhood

Point of Entry or How Crime Occurred

Example

    pried open front door, smashed wind-wing

Instrument or Means Used

Example

    handgun, knife, unknown pry tool

Where were occupants at time of offense?

Example

    at work, at school, on vacation

Victim's activity at time of offense

Example

    working as bank teller, jogging in park

Exact words used by suspect

Example

    "gimme the money"

Force or method used

Example

    shot victim, stabbed victim, punched him

Apparent motive

Examples

    personal or monetary gain, inflict bodily injury, revenge, sexual gratification, narcotics addiction, and accidental

Trademark or unique & unusual actions

Examples

      suspect wore ski mask, pried sliding door

Transportation used by suspect

Example

      car, truck, bicycle, walked

PRELIMINARY INVESTIGATION CHECKLIST

- Probable Cause - Stop, detention, arrest, search and seizure

- Arrest the Suspect - Don't overlook lawful arrests

- Locate Witnesses - If practical, canvass the neighborhood

- Interview Witnesses - Remember officers talk to everyone

- Protect the Crime Scene - Maintain original condition

- Interview the Suspect - Check department policy

- Note Taking - Note all pertinent findings & interviews

- Arrange for Forensic Sciences - Crime scene investigators

- Yield to Investigation - Document the arrival of detectives

- Complete the Report - The investigation isn't complete until the report is approved

SPECIFIC CRIME CHECKLISTS

Burglary

- Maintain Crime Scene - "Latent" fingerprints are invisible.

- Determine Crime - May be a repossession, children of the victim, roommates, or a false report.

- Determine Point of Entry - Account for suspect's actions from arrival to departure.

- Complete Listing of Loss - Detailed description and location in building.

- Check Exterior - Look for physical evidence or stolen property left behind.

- Crime Scene Investigation - Arrange for identification to work the scene.

- Canvass for Witnesses - Check the neighborhood for witnesses, stolen property, suspicious persons or vehicles.

- Enter stolen property into the computer system.

- Report - Document your preliminary investigation.

Child Abuse

- Check on the child's welfare - Depending on circumstance and law you may force entry into the home. Check on the child at school or have another officer on a later shift stop.

- Interview the child alone - Talk to the child separately from the parent or suspect. Get an explanation; does it make sense?

- Examine the victim - Look for bumps on his / her head, bruises, missing hair, burn marks, and ask about any complaint of pain.

- Check for other children / victims in the family.

- Interview Witnesses - Other family members, residents of the home, and neighbors.

- If a crime has occurred, PROTECT THE CHILD. Take custody of the victim, according to department policy.

- Reinterview the suspect - After arrest or seeing the child removed from the home, suspect's guilt often causes confession.

- Collect Evidence - Arrange for the crime scene investigation, photos, collect weapons, etc.

- Medical Examination - If necessary or possible, arrange for the child to be examined and then interview the physician.

- Notifications - Make necessary notifications, e.g. supervisor, county child abuse department, etc.

Child Molest

- Follow the basic steps outlined for child abuse.

- Develop a rapport with the victim.

- Determine the child's maturity level.

- Use terms the child is familiar with to describe body parts or activities (consider using a doll or ask the child to draw a picture).

- Consider a sexual assault medical examination if the time of occurrence is recent.

- Time of occurrence - Use holidays, school days, birthdays, etc. to help the child remember and to determine the date and time of occurrence.

- PROTECT THE CHILD - Notify your supervisor and take the child into protective custody.

Notes

Deaths

- Initial Response - Formulate your plan & communicate with other units responding.

- Mental Preparation - Control your emotions, prepare for what you are about to see; anticipate chaos.

- Arrival - Use appropriate tactical approach for the situation.

- Maintain the Crime Scene - Be alert for fragile evidence.

- Note Taking - Document the scene, conditions, physical evidence.

- Evaluate the Scene - Always consider the possibility of a homicide, suicide, or natural causes.

- Request Appropriate Assistance - Supervisor, coroner's office.

- Interviews - Try to find out what happened; interview witnesses, neighbors, etc.

- Dying Declaration - If the victim isn't dead, is a dying declaration appropriate?

- Report - Document your preliminary investigation.

Felony Assault

- Note Times - Record the time the call was received and the time of arrival on scene.

- Separate Parties - Calm the situation if necessary.

- First Aid - If necessary for the victim or call paramedics.

- Crime Scene - Observe the scene and protect evidence; note the condition of the room, etc.

- Locate Weapon - Isolate it; do not touch or move it unless an emergency circumstance require action. If you must move it, do it cautiously; it is primary evidence.

- Interview Victim & Witness - Do not take sides.

- Interrogate Suspect - If still present, otherwise put out appropriate radio broadcast.

- Arrest Suspect - If present and appropriate.

- Arrange for Photographs - Sometimes photographs can be taken a day or two later.

- Note Taking - Keep neat and accurate notes including times, names, evidence, injuries, and statements.

Robbery

- Initial Response - Formulate your plan and communicate with other responding units.

- Arrival - If an "in progress" call, follow appropriate tactical procedures.

- Maintain the Crime Scene - Be alert to fragile evidence.

- Interviews - Verify information from the initial broadcast and then conduct thorough interviews of victims and witnesses.

- Note Taking - Special concerns are weapon and suspect description.

- Arrange for Crime Scene Investigation.

- Notifications - Supervisor and investigation.

- Report - Document your preliminary investigation.

Sexual Assault

- Arrival - Record the time, weather conditions, and visibility.

- Locate Victim - Determine the victim's condition and need for immediate medical attention.

Notes

- Suspect Information - Get a description and direction of travel and notify adjacent units / agencies.

- Protect the Crime Scene - Remember, in a kidnap there are two or more crime scenes, and the victim's physical condition is evidence.

- Interview - Temper your interview, remembering what the victim has just experienced. Patience and sensitivity are important.

- Hospital - If appropriate, take the victim for examination and collection of evidence.

- Notifications - Make necessary notifications, e.g. supervisor and investigation.

- Report - Document your preliminary investigation.

Chapter 12

CORRECTIONS REPORT WRITING

PRINCIPLES OF A GOOD CORRECTIONS REPORT

Writing reports and completing forms are essential tasks of the correctional officer. Reports and forms are essential to the operation of a jail because they:

- Establish an accurate, cumulative record of occurrences within the facility

- Provide the jail administrator with information of which he/she must be aware

- Provide documentation that is important in the event of litigation.

A corrections report, by definition, is a formal presentation of facts. It is a written recollection of the writer and provides a permanent record of his/her actions, observations and discoveries. Since a report is a presentation, it may be reviewed by all elements in the criminal justice system, including inmates and their attorneys. It contains only facts, not judgments, innuendos or opinions.

A report is a legal document and therefore as a general rule is written for any unusual incident or situation or as documentation of any procedure or event that impacts on the safety and security of the facility and its occupants or the legality or constitutionality of department operations.

Reports in correctional facilities tend to fall into one of three different areas:

1. Reports completed by others, which jail staff must review for accuracy and completeness, such as court documents, visitor's logs, admission/release reports, etc. It is critical that the officer in this case know what sections must be completed and that proper signatures appear on the report.

2. Reports that the officer completes but requires no narrative information, such as; head counts, perimeter checks, cell and dorm checks, medication logs, etc. Unusual incidents or situations may be noted on these reports.

3. Reports that the officer completes which require narrative statements. These range from short remarks in the pass-down log to detailed descriptions of events/incidents. These reports tend to be the most difficult since they require the greatest report writing skills.

Written reports are, in many ways, like word pictures that must be carefully painted.

The key elements in a carefully painted work picture (report) are:

- Language that precisely conveys an action, observation or discovery

- Brevity (to the degree possible)

- Good form

SEVEN ESSENTIALS OF ALL GOOD REPORTS

To properly and completely relate an idea, incident or event, information and data must be collected which provides the answers to certain basic questions. These basic questions are known as the seven essentials of report writing, and are commonly referred to as WHO, WHAT, WHEN, WHERE, WHY, HOW and ACTION TAKEN.

WHO? Who was involved? Identify:

- All persons connected in any way with the occurrence (including all witnesses as well as those directly involved);

- Each individual should be identified in a manner that eliminates the possibility of confusion with another individual (i.e. for inmates, include: name, living quarters, assigned cellblock or cell numbers, dormitory/bed numbers, or other appropriate designations, and work assignment.

- Identify the staff by complete name and title.

WHAT? Provide a clear, unmistakable description of what happened. Ask the following:

- What took place that called for a report? Was it fighting, possession of contraband, attempting to escape or assault?

- What specific offense, if any, was committed?

- What are the elements of the offense?

- What was the object of the action?

The officer should also consider:

- What kind of damage was done?

- Was the value of the property lost, stolen or recovered?

- What evidence was left at the scene?

- What kinds of weapons or tools were used?

- Does further action need to be taken?

WHEN? What time, day, date; month and year did it happen?

- What time did it happen? State the hour and minute it happened only if known. ("I had just finished making my midnight rounds. It was 00:10 a.m. when I started and rounds take about 10 minutes to complete. I was walking toward the control room from B cellblock.")

- Refer to "approximate" time if the exact time is not known. Set out approximations within limits, such as between possible minutes within a single day, or between certain hours of one day and a subsequent day. (Between the hours of 8:00 a.m., March 3, 1995, and 3:00 p.m. on Saturday, March 4, 1995.)

- What month? What year? Name the day and date. This will help in the retrieval of past documentation. Never use indefinite expressions of time such as "last week", "yesterday" or "two days ago."

- Be specific and exact. Exactness in reporting time will maintain the chronological sequence and is essential when testimony is required. Errors in documenting correct time can taint the credibility of a factual report, and waste time in reconstructing events (sometimes under uncomfortable cross-examinations in court).

Additional points to consider when establishing "when" include:

- When was the infraction committed?

- When was the infraction discovered?

- Was/were the suspect(s) observed?

Notes

- How long did it take to commit the infraction?

- Did the inmate have enough time to dispose of the evidence?

WHERE? Where specifically did the incident happen in the jail?

- Note "identifiable" locations (i.e., "In the southeast corner of the dining room just in front of the commissary door.")

- Document the location of persons involved as well as important facts. (i.e., Inmate Johnson was standing directly in front of the commissary door. Inmate Floyd was behind him but obscured by Johnson?"

- Specify the position of the reporting officer as well as other officers during the incident. Also, note the position of all witnesses. ("I was in the dining room in the southwest corner by the fountain facing the southeast corner from which I could view the incident.")

- A guideline is to assume that the reporting officer is the only one with specific location referred to in the report or where certain items were found. Therefore, in describing a location or referencing a place where something (perhaps contraband) was found, do not assume any knowledge on the part of anyone else.

The officer should also consider:

- Where were the tools or weapons obtained?

- Where has a similar infraction been committed (inside the jail)?

HOW? How did it happen?

This can answer a vast array of questions about the occurrence and is very often the largest, most detailed portion of the report narrative. "How" questions should create a "word picture" of the happening in chronological order. In addition, specific "how" questions can help uncover serious gaps in jail security. Some examples of "how" questions include:

- How did the incident take place?

- How was the offense committed?

- How did the hacksaw blades get into the jail?

- How did the inmate in segregation obtain a book of matches?

- How did the marijuana get into the jail?

- How was the property or person attacked?

- How did the victim act and respond?

- How did the witness learn the facts?

WHY? Why did it happen? What was the motive?

Many times, this is the most difficult element in the report to determine. The following key issues will help the reporting officer "get to the bottom" of the occurrence and prevent false reporting.

State only the facts:

- A fact is that which an investigator has learned through the use of his five senses.

- A fact is that which the investigator (reporter) has heard, has seen, has tasted or has touched.

- Facts are the personal knowledge gained by the reporter (investigator) first-hand from the situation, through his senses. However, senses can be deceiving. Cocaine is not cocaine until a lab says it is cocaine. Our senses can be deceiving particularly when we have a predisposition to suspiciousness. What appears to be cocaine might be foot powder or vice versa.

Do not guess or include hearsay unless you qualify your statement:

- Hearsay is learned, second-hand by the reporter (investigator). It is something another person heard, saw, etc.

- Statements from other persons, even when they are eyewitnesses, are hearsay as far as a report is concerned. Identify who made a statement to you, being sure to qualify that the statement may not necessarily reflect fact.

Notes

COMMONLY MISSPELLED WORDS

abduction	dispatched	offense	sense
accelerate	disposition	official	sentence
accelerated	drunkenness	opinion	separate
accessories	effect	opportunity	separation
accident	embarrass		sergeant
accommodate	embezzlement	paid	serious
achievement	emergency	particular	sheriff
acquire	environment	patrolling	shining
acquitted	evidence	pedestrian	similar
affidavit	exaggerate	penalize	statute
alright	existence	performance	strangulation
altercation	existent	personal	studying
among	experience	personnel	subpoena
apparatus	explanation	possession	succeed
apparent	extortion	possible	succession
arguing		practical	suicide
argument	fascinate	precede	summons
arrest	forcible	precinct	surprise
arson	fraudulent	prejudice	surrender
assault		premises	surveillance
	height	prepare	suspect
belief	homicide	prevalent	suspicion
believe		principal	
beneficial	indict	principle	techniques
benefitted	interest	privilege	testimony
bureau	interrogate	probably	than
burglary	intimidation	procedure	their
	intoxication	proceed	then
category	investigation	profession	there
coercion	its (it's)	professor	they're
coming		prominent	thieves
commission	juvenile	prosecute	thorough
comparative		prostitution	to/too/two
complainant	larceny	pursue	traffic
conscious	led	pursuit	transferred
conspiracy	legal		trespassing
controversial	lieutenant	quiet	truancy
controversy	lose		
conviction	losing	receive	unnecessary
corpse		receiving	
counterfeit	marriage	recommend	vagrancy
criminal	marshal	referring	victim
	mere	repetition	villain
defendant		resistance	
define	necessary	rhythm	warrant
definitely		robbery	woman
definition	occasion		write
describe	occurred	sabotage	writing
description	occurrence	scene	
disastrous	occurring	seize	

ACTION TAKEN

What action did the officer take? What disposition was made of the evidence, inmate, victim and witnesses involved? The officer should be certain to include all action which has been taken and list any action which is pending, such as persons to be interviewed and an analysis of evidence.

- Did the officer summon help?

- Did he arrange for transport to the hospital or on-the-spot first aid?

- Did the officer handle the incident informally?

- Who was notified of the incident (a shift supervisor, another officer, or the jail administrator)?

- Was any evidence collected? If so, what was the disposition?

- Were any forms required to be completed or log entries made relative to the occurrence? If so, where were these reports sent and specifically, to whom?

The seven essential elements are key to development of an accurate and defensible report. Many reports are not defensible and are of little use due to poor preparation. Reports are often dismissed because of:

- Insufficient facts or evidence

- Insufficient relationship between text and action requested

- Inclusion of personal opinion

- Incident better handled informally

- Poorly organized statement of generalities rather than specifics

NOTE TAKING

Officers are not always able to write a report immediately after an incident has occurred. For instance:

- Medical emergencies requiring immediate transportation;

- Fire emergencies requiring evacuation and cleanup;

- Insufficient time to do complete reports prior to end of shift.

In situations like these, the officer must make a temporary record of the event until a formal report can be written. Notes can be used to refresh the officer's memory. Remember:

- Always carry a notebook

- Notes should cover the "seven essentials of a report"

- They should be made as soon as possible following the event

- Record only facts and observation, not opinions

- Reference all communication with others and reports filed

- Notes should include statements of participants and witnesses

- Where applicable, notes should include sketches of the scene and locations of people and important objects

- Note all evidence collected and its disposition

- If the situation warrants, have pictures taken, marked, and make note of them

- Record events in chronological order and give approximate times

- Number the pages of your notebook consecutively and do not remove any pages. Notebooks often serve as evidence and need to be maintained this way to protect the integrity of the record. When your notebook is full, do not discard it, but file it in a safe place in chronological order with your other notebooks.

PRESERVATION OF EVIDENCE

When handling evidence remember:

- Evidence should be picked up by the person who found it and not passed from person to person.

- Mark it. Either physically mark the object, attach a tag or label to it, store it in a marked container or in some other way to ensure that it is permanently identifiable.

- Note it. Note the means of marking and the physical description. Include serial numbers, model numbers, brand names, etc.

- Report it. Include a record of all evidence and its disposition in the appropriate reports.

- Document chain of evidence. A written record must be made each time the evidence passes from one person to another and of how the evidence is secured by each person. Generally there is no double jeopardy created by holding both administrative disciplinary proceedings and filing criminal charges. Therefore, jail officers must document evidence chain for possible criminal disposition of offense. But always check with legal advisors.

LOG ENTRIES

During the first year of service, a jail officer will literally make thousands of log entries. Such entries are the backbone of a jail's system of record keeping and basic documentation. During a lawsuit against individual officers or the county perhaps no other single type of documentation is as important as the carefully kept log. Several types of logs exist, depending upon the policies and procedures followed in the jail. Some of the more common types of logs include:

- **Daily Activity Log.** Usually kept in the control room or main post of the jail, this log documents the general flow of activity in the jail. It serves as a minute-by-minute diary of what at the time may seem to be inconsequential events (i.e., times of arrival by officers for shifts, when the meals arrived, time of physician's arrival for sick call, etc.). The Daily Activity Log is extremely useful as a "pass on" log for sharing information with other shifts. Some jails actually utilize a separate "pass on book".

- **Medical Log.** Many facilities keep a special log, which accompanies officers on rounds to administer medication. Such a log includes information such as the inmate's name, the name of the medication and dosage, time of administration and spaces for initials by the inmate and administering officer.

Notes

- **Transportation Log.** This serves as a record of all persons moved by vehicles outside the facility, dates and times, miles traveled, destination, purpose, odometer readings and related information. Many inmates allege assaults by officers during transport. Careful documentation is essential during this time.

- **Daily Sanitation/Security Inspection Log.** While basic sanitation and security inspections and their findings may be mentioned on the Daily Activity Log, some jails (particularly those under court order for sanitation/security violations) often find it useful to establish this separate form of documentation.

Additional specialized types of logs sometimes opted for by jail administration include tool and key logs, recreation equipment logs, recreation participant logs, mail logs, unit logs, administrative/disciplinary cell logs, etc. Each plays an integral part in the overall goal of a well-documented jail operation.

IMPORTANT!

- Be specific about the condition of inmates when making cell checks. A note about their mood or activity in which engaged is good practice. "Johnson in Cell #9 is reading on a bunk." "O.K." is Not an adequate log entry.

- Entries should reflect observations.

- Any and all unusual occurrences should be noted.

- Follow through! Officers who are going off duty should verbally summarize

DISCIPLINE REPORT WRITING PROCEDURES

The proper completion of a report is the first and most important part of the disciplinary process. Additionally, a good report improves the credibility of the reporting staff member, promotes uniformity and eliminates confusion.

The First Step

The first step in dealing with any inmate rule violation is always to take control of the situation. Staff members on the scene should take steps to restore and/or maintain order and security, and protect the safety of all staff and inmates.

Treatment of injuries or illness will always take precedent over the filing of reports. Serious or life-threatening situations will always be the first priority.

The Second Step - Preparing to Write

Many reports written by staff are simple enough that no special steps may be needed. At other times a degree of preparation will be necessary if the report is to be satisfactory. This may be the case if:

- The report is going to be very long

- There were a large number of staff and/or inmates involved

- The incident occurred over a long period of time, or involved several violations

- The incident was serious, as in an escape or serious assault

- The report may be needed by law enforcement personnel in an investigation, or as evidence in court

In such cases it will be necessary to organize the material before you begin writing the report. It is recommended that the following steps be taken:

- As the incident evolves, make an effort to observe times, locations, participants, etc.

- Immediately afterwards, make notes. It is permissible to verify some information (such as times, etc.) with other staff members who were involved.

- Write the report as soon after the incident as possible. If necessary, ask your supervisor to help arrange this. Do not leave it for the end of shift for convenience's sake.

- If it is a long or complex report, create an outline to work from. If you have trouble with outlines, try writing down each thing that occurred in order and numbering them.

ELEMENTS OF A GOOD REPORT

Generally, the report should include the basic elements who, what, when, where, why and how. Here are a few specific principles to follow when completing a report.

Notes

- **Ensure chronological order.** The report should first indicate the initial time and date of the incident. The events in the report should then be documented in the order of their occurrence. Other specific times should be noted throughout the report when relevant.

- **The report should be clear, concise and detailed.** The report should leave no question in the reader's mind as to what exactly transpired during the incident. Information that has no relevance to the incident, or to the violation being described, should not be included.

- **List all persons present during the incident.** All persons involved in the incident should be listed in the body of the report. This includes all staff, inmates, and anyone who may have witnessed the event.

- **State who was notified.** It is important to include in your report when your supervisor was notified of the incident. If the incident included the need for medical attention, note the times medical staff was notified and the instructions they gave. If notification of an outside agency is required, note the times and, if known, the names of the individuals contacted.

- **Reference supplemental reports.** List the numbers of any additional reports from other staff concerning the incident. Report any other documentation completed by other agencies.

- **Document physical evidence.** List and describe physical evidence collected for future use during disciplinary hearings. Physical evidence may include such items as a broken cup, photographs of vandalism, a weapon, or contraband. If an item of physical evidence is turned over to a law enforcement agency, list the case number; name of the officer who took possession and the date/time the officer took possession.

- **Describe any use of restraints or medical equipment.** Include the time applied, time checked, time removed, and officer's involved.

- **Document medical attention.** Following any altercation involving an inmate or staff member, medical attention must be offered and the offer must be documented in the report.

- **When possible, quote the inmate.** Quoting the inmate leaves the reader with little doubt as to what the officer alleges the inmate stated. This is especially important when the charge will include insolence, threats or refusing direct orders. Do not, however, put anything in quotation marks unless you are absolutely sure they are the exact words used.

- **Reports should be factual.** The writer's personal opinions or interpretations should be left out.

- **Make sure there are facts in the report that support the violation you believe occurred.** A supervisor who will determine, based on the facts contained in the report, if a disciplinary charge is warranted and exactly what it will be, will review the report. The elements of the violation must therefore be evident in the report.

- **Identify the report as misconduct, rather than merely an investigative report.** Do not state a specific charge in the body of the report. Include instead the following sentence as the last line: "This report is being referred to the shift supervisor for possible disciplinary charges."

- **Proofread the report.** Before turning a report in, check for spelling, punctuation and sentence construction. Be sure the report is clear and easy to understand. Since it is usually difficult to accurately proofread your own work, you may want to have another employee do this for you.

CHARACTERISTICS OF AN UNSATISFACTORY REPORT

When a violation proceeding results in an inmate being found not guilty, it is frequently due to the content of the report. A report could be considered un-satisfactory for any of the following reasons:

- The content of the report is unclear and/or unorganized.

- There are discrepancies in the times, dates, locations and/or persons involved in the incident.

- The report does not accurately describe all aspects of the incident.

- The facts are not sufficient to meet elements of the violation.

FILING CHARGES

Filing disciplinary charges is the responsibility of the shift supervisor. The procedure is as follows:

- **Read the report carefully.** Check the quality of the report. It should be clear and well written, with correct spelling, grammar etc. and be easy to read and understand. If it is not, have it corrected by the officer.

- **Identify the rule or rules violated.** Look for acts specifically identified in the report that corresponds with the elements of a particular violation. Disciplinary charges must be based upon the facts contained in the report. If it is clear that no violation took place, treat the report as a non-disciplinary investigative report. If it appears that a violation occurred, but the facts in the report are unclear or insufficient to support a charge, discuss the report with the reporting employee. If the report can be improved, the employee should make the corrections and re-submit the report.

- **Complete a "Hearing Summary" form.** Charges are "filed" when a supervisor designates this on a Hearing Summary form. A separate form must be used for each charge that is filed from a particular report/incident. This is because those charges on which an inmate is found not guilty cannot be placed in his/her file along with those on which s/he is found guilty. Avoid "loading up" a report with charges. In most cases, charging an inmate with the most obvious or important violation apparent in the report is appropriate. It is perfectly acceptable, however, to file multiple charges when the circumstances warrant them.

- **Send major misconduct reports** to the Disciplinary Supervisor.

- **Log minor misconduct reports.** A log should be maintained at the facility for minor misconduct reports. The purpose of the log is to help supervisors insure that reports are heard within the prescribed time frames, and to prevent reports from being lost or handled with out proper hearing.

Chapter 13

SUSPECT DESCRIPTIONS

SUSPECTS

Many descriptions in police reports are so vague and general they could apply to almost anyone. Victims and witnesses are more likely to recall information if they are prompted by the officer.

It is essential the description of suspects be as detailed and complete as possible. Complete, individual descriptions will enhance the investigation and prosecution.

Suspect Description Checklist

- Generally, start the description at the top (suspect's head) and work down (suspect's feet).

- Sex: Male or female

- Race: Descent is an identifier. For example:

White	Black
Hispanic or Latino	Indian or Native American

  Asian or specific country of origin

- Age: Give the exact age if possible; if not, use an approximation, e.g. 18-23 yrs.

- Height: Use your stature as a gauge; however, don't tell the informant your height. Ask, "taller than I am or shorter?" If necessary use an approximation with a range of 3" to 4" (5'8" to 6'0", for example).

- Weight: Same as height; ask the witness to compare to your size; then make the estimate with a range of 25 lbs. or less, e.g. 140-165 lbs.

Notes

- Build

Thin	Athletic
Small	Medium
Stocky	Heavy
Muscular	Overweight

- Hair Color

Blond	Salt / pepper
Light brown	Bald / shaved
Brown	Streaked
Black	Gray
Dyed	Bleached
Red	

- Hair Style

Crew cut, butch	Corn rows
Perms	Balding
Braids	Receding
Pony-tail	Wig / Toupee
Military style	Afro
Rolls or buns	Over Ears
Collar length	On collar
Sideburns	Shoulder length
Left part	Right Part
No part	Combed Straight Back

- Eyes (Describe the color, shape, and any special conditions.)

Blue	Blood shot
Brown	Watery
Hazel	Missing
Green	Glasses
Black	Cross-eyed

- Facial Hair

Ask if the suspect had facial hair, rather than asking if he had a beard or mustache. Be certain you and the witness have the same meanings for each term.

Beards	(cover the face with whiskers)
Goatee	(covers the chin)
Sideburns	(see hair style, hair in front of the ear, extending down from the hair line)
Mustache	(whiskers above the upper lip)
Fu Manchu	(the moustache droops downward)
Handlebar	(the moustache is waxed and turns up)
Pencil thin	(thick, thin, or bushy)

- Complexion

Light	Dark
Medium	Light brown
Olive	Medium
Reddish	Dark brown
Freckles	Acne / pimples
Birth Marks	Red spots
Moles / Warts	Flaky Skin

- Scars
  Location, design, and size

- Peculiarities - anything to differentiate the suspect from other people.

Gold teeth	Speech problems
False teeth	Slurred speech
Color of teeth	Regional accent
Braces	Foreign accent
Hair Lip	Unable to speak
Limp	Phrases
Cane / crutches	Stutter
Posture	Whisper
Body Odor	Lisp
Blindness	Nervous mannerisms
Mental capacity	

Notes

- Teeth / Missing body part
  Missing body part or facial disfiguration

  Amputations - fingers, etc.

- Clothing

Ask generic questions, rather than specific questions.

Incorrect

Was he wearing a baseball cap?

Correct

Was he wearing a hat?

- Style of Clothing
  Western   Formal
  Color   Length
  Private School   Costume
  Armed Services Postal Service
  City / county employee

- Type of Shoes
  Boots   Pumps
  Sandals   Tennis
  Slippers   Heels
  Specialty

- Gang Jewelry

- Tattoo
  Location   Words / letters
  Design / pattern Names
  Colors   Size

Chapter 14

SPELLING

Misspelled words confuse the reader, change the meaning of the words, and make the officer appear careless, stupid, and incompetent. The following are tips to improve your spelling:

SPELLER'S JOURNAL

When you get a report back with misspelled words, write those in the back of your notebook. We use the same words over and over; soon, you'll correctly spell those words.

DICTIONARY

When in doubt, always use a dictionary to verify spelling and meaning.

SPELLER / DIVIDER

Speller / dividers are pocket sized books that list the words correctly spelled. They don't have any definitions. Most officers know what the word means, just not how to spell it.

THESAURUS

A thesaurus is a book of synonyms, words with similar meanings. Use by police officers improves spelling and makes reports more interesting.

MISSPELLERS DICTIONARY

If you have trouble finding correctly spelled words in a dictionary, try a Misspellers Dictionary. The words are listed incorrectly spelled, followed by the correct spelling, e.g. newmonia / pneumonia.

ELECTRONIC SPELLERS

There are hand-held battery-powered electronic spellers available. The more sophisticated models include a dictionary and thesaurus.

PROOFREADING

Proofread your own work or have someone read it for you. Proofreading will greatly reduce the spelling errors.

HOMONYMS

Homonyms are words that sound alike, have different meanings, and are spelled differently. Officers should learn the difference and use the correctly spelled word.

Beat / beet	Presence / presents
Boar / bore	Principal / principle
Board / bored	Pride / pried
Bread / bred	Rain / reign / rein
Break / brake	Raise / rays / raze
Bridal / bridle	Rap / wrap
Buy / by / bye	Real / reel
Capital / capitol	Right / rite / write
Ceiling / sealing	Road / rode / rowed
Cent / sent / scent	Role / roll
Cereal / serial	Sail / sale
Cite / sight / site	Scene / seen
Chord / cord	Seam / seem
Corps / corpse	Seam / seem
Council / counsel	Sense / cents
Current / currant	Serf / surf
Dear / deer	Shear / sheer
Hole / Whole	Shone / shown
Idle / idol	Soar / sore
Its / it's	Sole / soul
Knew / new	Stairs / stares
Knot / not	Stake / steak
Know / no	Stationary / stationery
Liable / libel	Steal / steel
Lain / lane	Straight / strait
Lessen / lesson	Tail / tale
Lie / lye	Taught / taut
Loan / lone	Team / teem
Made / maid	Tear / tier
Maybe / may be	Their / there / they're
Meat / meet	Throne / thrown
Medal / meddle	Through / threw
Muscle / mussel	Tied / tide
Naval / navel	To / too / two
Oar / or / ore	Toe / tow

Ordinance / ordnance	Vain / vane / vein
Pail / pale	Vale / veil
Pain / pane	Vial / vile
Pair / pare / pear	Wail / whale
Pause / paws	Waist / waste
Peace / piece	Wait / weight
Peal / peel	Waived / waved
Peer / pier	Way / weigh
Pedal / peddle	Weak / week
Plain / plane	Wear / where
Pray / prey	Wholly / holey / holy

ABBREVIATIONS

Three Rules for Abbreviations

1. Spell out all titles except Mr., Mrs., Mmes, Dr., and St. (saint, not street).

2. Spell out Street, Road, Park, Company and similar words used as part of a proper name or title.

3. Spell out Christian names (William, not Wm.).

Standard Abbreviations

Dates

Jan.	Feb.	Mar.	Apr.
May	June	Jul.	Aug.
Sept.	Oct.	Nov.	Dec.

Mon.	Tues.	Wed	Thurs.
Fri	Sat	Sun	

1st	6th
2nd	7th
3rd	8th
4th	9th
5th	10th

Time

Yr. / Year	Yrs. / Years
Mo. / Month	Mos. / Months
Wk. / Week	Wks. / Weeks
Hr. / Hour	Hrs. / Hours
Min. / Minute	Mins. / Minutes
Sec. / Second	Secs. / Seconds

Measurement

In. / Inch	Ft. / Feet / foot
Yd. / Yard	Mi. / Mile
Gr. / Gram	Kg. / Kilogram
Km. / Kilometer	W. / Width
Lb. / Pound	Lbs. / Pounds
Oz. / Ounce	Wt. / Weight
Doz. / Dozen	L. / Length
Hgt. / Height	Meas. / Measurement

Common Abbreviations

Admin.	Administration
APB	All Points Bulletin
AOA	Assist Outside Agency
AKA	Also Known As
Amt.	Amount
Approx.	Approximate
Bur.	Bureau
Arr.	Arrest
ATL	Attempt to Locate
Asst.	Assistant
Atty.	Attorney
Att.	Attempt
Bldg.	Building
BPL	Birthplace
Burg.	Burglary
Cauc.	Caucasian
Capt.	Captain
CDL	California Drivers License
Cen.	Central
COP	Chief of Police
Chan.	Channel
COL	Colonel
Co.	Company
Constr.	Construction
Cvt.	Convertible
Ct.	Court
DOB	Date of Birth

DOA	Dead on Arrival
Def.	Defendant
Dept.	Department
Deg.	Degree
Det.	Detective
DMV	Dept. of Motor Vehicles
Descp.	Description
Dir.	Director
Div.	Division
Dist.	District
Dr.	Doctor
DBA	Doing Business As
DWI	Driving While Intoxicated
DL	Drivers License
DUI	Driving Under the Influence
E / B	Eastbound
Encl.	Enclosure
Engrs.	Engineers
Ex.	Example
Exec.	Executive
Fed.	Federal
Frt.	Freight
Ga.	Gauge
GB	General Broadcast
Govt.	Government
Hdq.	Headquarters
HV.	High Voltage
Hwy.	Highway
Hosp.	Hospital
ID	Identification
Inf.	Informant
Insp.	Inspector
Junc.	Junction
Jr.	Junior
Juv.	Juvenile
LKA	Last Known Address
L	Left
LF	Left Front
LH	Left Hand
LR	Left Rear
Lic.	License
Lt.	Lieutenant
Lt.Col.	Lieutenant Colonel
Maj.	Major
Mgr.	Manager

Notes

Mfg.	Manufacturing
Max.	Maximum
Mech.	Mechanical
Med.	Medium
Memo	Memorandum
MI	Middle Initial
Misd.	Misdemeanor
MO	Modus Operandi
NATB	Natn'l Auto Theft Bureau
NCIC	Natn'l Crime Info.Center
NFD	No Further Description
NA	Not Applicable
NMN	No Middle Name
N/B	Northbound
No.	Number
Nos.	Numbers
Numb.	Numbered
Off.	Officer / official
Opp.	Opposite
Org.	Organization
Pkg.	Package
P.	Page
PP.	Pages
Pass.	Passenger
PIN	Permanent ID Number
Pcs.	Pieces
Pt.	Pint
Pl.	Place
POE	Place of Entry
POI	Point of Impact
PO	Police Officer / Probation Officer
Qty.	Quantity
Qt.	Quart
R	Right
Recd.	Received
Req.	Required
Rd.	Road
RF	Right Front
RR	Right Rear / Rural Route / Railroad
Sch.	School
Sect.	Section
Ser.	Serial
Sgt.	Sergeant

S / B	Southbound
Subj.	Subject
Supt.	Superintendent
Sur.	Surface
Sym.	Symbol
Tbsp.	Tablespoon
Tech.	Technical
TT	Teletype
Tran.	Transportation
Treas.	Treasurer
Univ.	University
Unk.	Unknown
VIN	Vehicle ID Number
Vet.	Veterinarian / Veteran
Vil.	Village
Vol.	Volume
Wpn.	Weapon
Whsle.	Wholesale

Suspect Abbreviations

List suspect abbreviations in the following order:

- Race

- Gender

- Age

Example

WFA   or   White - female - adult

BMA   or   Black - male - adult

Chapter 15

PENMANSHIP

Most police departments use a "one-write" system. The officer's handwritten report is the original source document. Reports should be neat and legible.

Tips to Improve Penmanship:

- Reports should be block printed in capital letters.

- Lettering Guides - The LawTech Report Writing Templates are frequently used to insure uniform block lettering.

- Traffic and crime scene templates are used to draw specific items.

- Pens - use a larger barrel pen to improve your handwriting.

- Portable Typewriters - battery-operated electronic typewriters are available for approximately $125.00. Officers carry them in the patrol car and type their reports.

- Lap-top Computers - Some agencies have purchased lap-top computers and software programs for report writing.

Chapter 16

GLOSSARY OF TERMS

Adjective

An adjective modifies or describes a noun or a pronoun.

Adverbs

An adverb modifies or describes a verb, adjective, or another adverb.

Antecedent

The word or group of words to which a pronoun refers.

Appositive

A substantive set beside another substantive and signifying the same thing.

Collective Nouns

Use either singular or plural pronouns with collective nouns, depending on the sense of the sentence.

Comma Splice

The use of a comma, instead of a coordinating conjunction or a semicolon, between the two independent clauses of a compound sentence.

Complement

A word or group of words used to complete the sense of a verb. The complement of a transitive verb is an object, (completes the action).

Complex Sentence

One that consists of one independent clause and one or more dependent clauses.

Compound Sentence

One that consists of two or more independent clauses.

Conjunction

Connects words, phrases, or clauses in a sentence.

Dependent Clause

A group of words that has a subject and a finite verb that depends on a larger structure by a relative pronoun or by a subordinating conjunction.

Finite Verb

A verb that is fix or limited by its form in person, number and tense.

Gerund

A verbal that is formed from a verb, but functions as a noun.

Infinitive

A word that is formed from a verb but that functions in the sentence as a noun, an adjective, or an adverb.

Modifier

A word, phrase, or clause that limits, specifies, qualifies, or describes another word.

Noun

The name of a person, place, or thing.

Noun Clause

A dependent clause that can serve almost every function that a noun or pronoun or noun phrase can serve.

Noun Phrase

A noun or a pronoun and all of its modifiers, if any.

Parallelism

A grammatical principle where words, phrases, or clauses joined in a pair or in a series must be of the same kind.

Participle

A verbal that is formed from a verb but functions as an adjective.

Passive Verb

The form that a predicate verb takes when we want to indicate that the subject of the sentence is the receiver, not the doer, of the action (passive voice).

Preposition

Links or shows the relationship of a noun or pronoun to some other word in the sentence.

Pronoun

Takes the place of noun.

Run-on Sentence

Two or more independent clauses without any punctuation or coordinating conjunction.

Semantics

The branch of linguistics that deals with the study of the meanings of words.

Sentence

A group of words containing a subject (DOER) and a verb (ACTION) and expressing a complete thought.

Sentence Fragment

A sentence that does not have a complete thought.

Syntax

The branch of grammar that deals with the study of how words are put together to form meaningful phrases or clauses.

Tense

The aspect of a verb that indicates time: past, present, and future.

Voice

A change in verb form to indicate whether the subject acts (active voice) or is acted upon (passive voice).

APPENDIX

CHAPTER REVIEW QUESTIONS
AND
PRACTICAL APPLICATION EXERCISES

SAMPLE POLICE REPORTS

SAMPLE NOTES

Chapter 1

INTRODUCTION TO REPORT WRITING

1. A report is any written document, recorded on a departmental form, and kept as a permanent record.
   T   F

2. Arrest reports factually record the circumstances leading to the arrest of a suspect for a specific crime.
   T   F

3. An arrest report includes the probable cause for the stop, detention, arrest, and disposition of the suspect.
   T   F

4. Crime reports document the facts of an event showing a crime occurred.   T   F

5. The report must include the elements of the crime.   T   F

6. Reports are used to coordinate the officers' activities during an investigation.   T   F

7. Reports are used to compare past and current events to determine modus operandi and identify suspects.
   T   F

8. Crime reports are available to the press.   T   F

9. Reports are a resource for officer evaluation.   T   F

10. Police reports may be read by administrators, attorneys, insurance companies, and judges.   T   F

Chapter 2

CHARACTERISTICS OF A GOOD REPORT

1. There are six characteristics to a well-written report.   T   F

2. Accurate reports conform exactly to the facts.   T   F

3. Clear means the report is plain or evident to the reader; the meaning is unmistakable.   T   F

4. Reports must have all the necessary parts and include the who, what, when, where, why, and how. T   F

5. Concise means to express all the necessary information in as few words as possible.   T   F

6. A fact is something real and presented objectively and can be proven or disproved.   T   F

7. Objective police reports are not influenced by emotion, personal prejudice, or personal opinion. T   F

Chapter 3

THE BUILDING BLOCKS IN THE
REPORT WRITING PROCESS

1. An officer's interview of a victim, witness, or suspect is generally the first block in the report writing process. T F

2. Communication is the transfer of ideas resulting in an exchange of information. T F

3. Three types of non-verbal communications are: gestures, facial expression, and body language. T F

4. Five types of verbal communication are: one-way, two-way, oral-in person, oral-telephone, and written. T F

5. The Three Step Interview Method includes: subject tells the story, subject retells the story and the officer takes notes, and officer reads his notes to the informant. T F

6. Interrogations are interviews of suspects in crimes. T F

7. The problems with tape recording field notes are: equipment malfunction and too much unnecessary information is captured. T F

8. Notes are brief notations concerning specific events that are recorded while fresh in the officer's mind and used to prepare a report. T F

9. The scratch outline contains a key sentence and supporting points. T F

10. Use the scratch outline to organize information before writing the report. T F

Chapter 4

CHRONOLOGICAL ORDER

Directions: The following facts are pertinent to a residential burglary report. Read each statement and decide the correct chronological order for the narrative of the police report.

Place the #1 by the first fact, #2 by the second and so on until all statements have been put in order.

To help you follow the correct chronological order, when you arrived you first spoke to the victim Mr. Collins.

FACTS:

You are working day patrol and are assigned a report of a residential burglary. You are to see Mr. Wilbur NMN Collins at his house, located at 428 W. Hill St., Santa Ana, 92702. His phone is (714) 538-9668.

Mr. Collins' DOB is 1-22-52 and he works at 11451 Skypark Circle, Irvine, 96780. His phone number is (714) 545-3245 and he works Monday through Friday from 8 a.m. to 5 p.m. He's an engineer.

Mr. Collins neighbor, John Wesley Harding, lives at 430 W. Hill, Santa Ana 92702, phone (714) 538-5683. He's a retired fireman.

STATEMENTS:

_____ Mr. Harding said he didn't think he'd seen the car before, but would recognize both the car and the subject if he saw them again.

_____ When Collins came home at 12:15 p.m. the front door was open.

_____ The interior of Collins's house was ransacked. His RCA color television is missing from the family room. The set has a wood grain cabinets, 19" picture tube, serial number 416025 and is valued at $250.00.

_____ At 12:00 Collins's neighbor, Mr. Harding, called Collins at work. Harding told Collins there was a suspicious person at Collins's house.

_____ Mr. Collins locked all the windows and doors of his single family residence and left for work at 0730 hrs. this morning.

_____ Mr. Harding was mowing his front lawn at 11:30 a.m. when he saw a blue, 1974 VW Bug 2 door pull up in front of Collins's house.

_____ Collins found a screwdriver with a standard blade, about 3/8" wide, and a yellow plastic handle on the patio by the sliding glass door to his bedroom.

_____ The suspect was wearing blue slacks, a white shirt, and a necktie.

_____ Collins's sliding glass door was ajar and had been pried open. He went outside onto the patio.

_____ When Mr. Harding went back outside the subject was gone and so was the car. Collins's front door was open.

_____ Harding saw the suspect, a white male about 16-18 yrs. old, 5'10" tall, 165 lbs., with brown curly hair, get out of the VW, and walk up to Collins's front door.

_____ The suspect rang the door bell and when no one answered, walked around to the back of Collins's house.

_____ An envelope from the Tropicana Hotel in Las Vegas containing $400.00 (two 100's, two 50's, and five 20's) is missing from the master bedroom dresser drawer.

_____ Harding went into his house and called Collins.

Chapter 5

FIRST vs. THIRD PERSON STYLE

Directions: Determine if the sentence is first (F) or third person (T).

1.　The undersigned officer caught the suspect at Fifth and Main.　F　T

2.　While I was pursuing the alleged burglar, I was joined by Sgt. Randall.　F　T

3.　The victim asked me when he should call for further information.　F　T

4.　Lt. Green returned the report to this officer.　F　T

5.　Officer Gannon and this officer interviewed the victim.　F　T

6.　My partner and I arrested the suspect at 0430 hours.　F　T

7.　Assigned officer responded to the scene.　F　T

8.　When the children got lost, they asked me for directions.　F　T

9.　Officer Malloy discovered the gun in the driveway.　F　T

10.　While I continued to check for a witness, Officer Reed collected the evidence.　F　T

Chapter 6

CLEAR AND CONCISE WRITING STYLE

ACTIVE VOICE WRITING STYLE

Exercise #1

Directions: Determine if these sentences are active or passive voice. Use A for active and P for passive.

_____

It was determined by me the car was stolen.

_____

The sergeant called a squad meeting.

_____

Several witnesses were interviewed by Attorney Daniels.

_____

The report was written by him.

_____

Detective Peterson found the revolver on the floor.

_____

Exercise #2

Directions: Determine if these sentences are active or passive voice. If they are passive, rewrite them in the active voice.

1.   The monthly crime summary was completed by Chief Bowman and submitted to the city council.

          _____

          _____

2.   The suspect was searched and handcuffed by Officer Logan.

          _____

          _____

3.   On June 25th, Stein was arrested by Secret Service Agents.

_____

_____

4.   The officer was told by the sergeant to rewrite the report.

_____

_____

5.   The report of Officer Ramirez was approved by the sergeant.

_____

_____

6.   The unidentified victim was strangled by the suspect.

_____

_____

7.   It was discovered by me that the suspect had escaped through the back door.

_____

_____

8.   After being telephoned by the suspect, the victim withdrew her complaint.

_____

_____

Modifiers

Exercise #3

Directions: Locate and underline the misplaced or incorrect modifiers in the following sentences. Then correct the errors; in some cases you may have to rewrite the sentence.

1.   The sergeant told me they need someone who could type badly.

_____

2.   Upon searching the suspect, he became hostile.

_____

3.   Officer Smith was allowed to leave the first one to finish the test.

_____

4.   In the victim's closet which she seldom wore untouched by the intruder were many beautiful dresses.

_____

5.   Backup officers arrived and assisting in controlling the suspect.

_____

6.   The officer followed the suspect closely.

_____

7.   The department bought shiny, new police cars.

_____

8.   I bought a car from a used car dealer with a leaky radiator.

_____

9.   After running six blocks, the bus pulled away as I reached it.

_____

10.   The stolen car was taken to the police garage to be held for the detectives by the Ace Towing Company.

_____

11.   Anyone who reads the log frequently will notice that many officers are now handling more calls.

_____

12.   The Chief was a college graduate, articulate, and egotistical.

_____

Agreement: Pronoun and Subject/Verb

Exercise #4

Directions: Circle the antecedent in each sentence.

1. Margot said, "I need directions to the lake."

2. The girls went to eat their lunch.

3. Sam wrote the letter but can't find it now.

4. Julie and Nancy can't find the spice they need for the pie.

5. The boys did the work themselves.

Exercise #5

Directions: Circle the antecedent in each sentence. Then rewrite the sentence to make it less confusing.

1. Officer Paul told Officer Johnson he couldn't find his report.

   _____

   _____

2. The sergeant told the citizen he could file a report.

   _____

   _____

3. The officer said, "If you want him arrested, try putting the cuffs on."

   _____

   _____

4. The Chief told the councilman the officers wanted him to resign.

   _____

   _____

5.   There were customers in the bank with the robbers. They were scared.

_____

_____

Exercise #6

Directions: Circle the correct form of the verbs in the blanks.

1.   Neither the suspect nor his accomplices was/were caught.

2.   New developments in technology mean/means a different career for police officers.

3.   The detectives or the patrol officer was/were first to arrive.

4.   The mayor's use of crime statistics make/makes him sound important.

5.   The jury has/have reached a verdict.

Deadwood Words

Exercise #7

Directions: Replace the following words or phrases with a simple word or phrase.

1. adjacent to   _____

2. a large portion of   _____

3. altercation   _____

4. transport   _____

5. with a minimum of delay _____

6. customary   _____

7. observe   _____

8. contacted   _____

9. responded to   _____

10. commence _____

11. in short supply _____

12. exit _____

13. for the reason that _____

14. prior to _____

15. on account of the fact that _____

16. indicate _____

17. it should be noted that _____

18. endeavor _____

19. was of the opinion that _____

20. resides _____

Word Meanings

Exercise #8

Directions: Circle the correct form of the word in the blanks.

1. The sergeant thought the Chief was already/all ready at the meeting.

2. The Chief was already/all ready for the meeting.

3. When/As I arrived the suspect was still in the car.

4. The suspect asked to speak to his legal counsel/council .

5. Upon/When I arrived both suspects were in the police car.

Chapter 7

RULE OF GRAMMAR, PUNCTUATION, AND MECHANICS

Adjectives and Adverbs

Exercise #1

Directions: Circle the adjective or adverb in the following sentences.

1.   The victim was quickly moved to a hospital.

2.   The injured suspect was treated at the scene.

3.   The officer tackled the tall suspect.

4.   The male suspect yelled at the victim.

5.   The suspect ran very quickly.

Sentences

Comma Splice, Run-on or Fused, and Fragments

Exercise #2

Directions: Label each of the following sentences as (F) = fragment, (R) = run-on; (C) = comma splice. Rewrite the sentences and correct the faulty sentence structure.

_____1. Each of us did the assignment, we bought new books.

_____

_____

_____ 2. Handled the situation well.

_____

_____

_____3. If I could live anywhere in the world, I would still choose the United States, sometimes we don't realize how fortunate we Americans are.

_____

_____

_____4. The house on the hill belonged to the suspect he bought it from the victim.

_____

_____

Exercise #3

Directions: Rewrite the sentences and correct the faulty sentence structure.

1. Until the detectives were able to sift through the evidence and learn the truth.

_____

_____

2. The two officers left at 5:00 p.m., what time is it now?

_____

_____

3. Is on the other side of the street.

_____

_____

4. When the attorney was shown the evidence that was being presented against his client and realized the helplessness of his case.

_____

_____

5. Mike found the trail when he reached the mouth of the canyon.

_____

_____

6.   The dog dug a hole under the roses, he buried his bone there.

_____

_____

Punctuation

Apostrophes, Possessives, Colon, Semi-colon, Comma, Dash,
Exclamation Point, Parenthesis, Periods, & Question Marks

Exercise #4

Directions: Circle the correct answer in the following sentences.

1.   The officer <u>couldn't/could'nt</u> arrest the suspect.

2.   The Chief <u>did'nt/didn't</u> return this afternoon.

3.   Officer Smith picked up <u>Brad's/Brads'</u> notepad.

4.   Officer <u>Jones'/Jones's</u> police car was dirty.

5.   The <u>officers'/officers's</u> guns were inspected last week.

6.   The <u>women's/womens'</u> lockers are the same as the <u>men's/mens'</u>.

Exercise #5

If the sentence is correct, write "correct" in the blank. If the sentence is not correct, rewrite it in the blank or make the necessary correction to the typed sentence in the textbook.

1.   The sergeant assigned officers to the following locations: the pier, the alley, and the front of the building.

     _____

     _____

2.   The rules and regulations serve two purposes, they protect the department and protect the officer.

     _____

     _____

3.   The sergeant briefed the troops he read all the pertinent material.

     _____

     _____

4.   The department is hiring more officers; therefore, all current officers will have new assignments.

     _____

     _____

5.   The sergeants from three details are Brown, Robbery; Smith, Training; and Davis, Homicide.

     _____

     _____

6.   After baking mother did the laundry.

     _____

     _____

7.   In his pockets the suspect had a switchblade a vial of a white powdery substance about a yard of nylon string and a roach clip.

     _____

     _____

8. This exercise for example helps in punctuating sentences correctly.

    _____

    _____

9. The prosecuting attorney asked "Did you find the weapon at the scene?"

    _____

    _____

10. The accident happened in front of Tomaine Tommy's Bar 1000 South Retch Street Your Town California.

    _____

    _____

11. The victim, witness, and officer these people attended the line-up.

    _____

    _____

12. The robbery and theft laws are between pages 1230-1235.

    _____

    _____

13. Help, I can't get out of the car.

    _____

    _____

14. The suspect had been smoking a joint marijuana cigarette.

    _____

    _____

15. The cashier estimated the loss was fifty dollars ($50).

    _____

    _____

16.   The deputy arrested the suspect

_____

_____

17.   Why did the deputy arrest the suspect?

_____

_____

18.   Lt Davis is also in the National Guard

_____

_____

19.   There are three tests: (1) written exam, (2) physical agility, and (3) interview.

_____

_____

Mechanics

Capitalization, Hyphens, Numbers, Quotation Marks, & Underlining

Exercise #6

Directions: Read the following sentences and if necessary make corrections. If the sentence is correct, write the letter "C" at the end of the sentence.

1.   Officer Jones is transferring to the phoenix police department.

2.   he should be very happy in phoenix.

3.   The Chief said, "No one has been arrested."

4.   The Chief transferred lt. Harry McClure to Records.

5.   The court order granted inmate Ratchford pro-per privileges.

6.   The City Council approved twenty two new positions.

7. Three hundred people were arrested over the holiday weekend.

8. The victim was 2 years 5 months old.

9. The suspect had $351.77 in his pocket.

10. The suspect took approximately $100.00 and ran out the door.

11. The city has 45,679 residents.

12. The Chief said, I'm going to retire on May 1st.

13. The officer thought the suspect was "conwise".

14. All new lieutenants should read, Megatrends.

15. The victim said she was watching Days of Our Lives when she heard the shot.

Chapter 8

PARAGRAPHING

Directions: Read the key sentence. Use the words in the word list to write five telling sentences. Arrange those sentences into a paragraph.

Word List

victim	park	old
purse	alone	keys
walking	woman	hid
money	ran	broke
grabbed	took	drugs
cop	fell	caught
identify	felled	jail

Key Sentence: Officer Spence arrested suspect Ralph Green for theft.

Write five telling sentences.

1. _____

2. _____

3. _____

4. _____

5. _____

Arrange the sentences into a paragraph.

Chapter 9

REPORT EDITING

1.   The use of adjectives improves reports.   T   F

2.   Related words should be near each other in sentences.   T   F

3.   Eliminate phrases; try to use single words.   T   F

4.   Try to use the most concise form of a word.   T   F

5.   Try to eliminate the phrases "of a" and "such an".   T   F

6.   Try to eliminate words ending in "tive' and "tion".   T   F

7.   Use suffixes and prefixes.   T   F

8.   Try to eliminate the word "that" from most sentences.   T   F

9.   Try to eliminate the word "then" from most sentences.   T   F

10.   Try to eliminate phrases like "which is" and "who is".   T   F

Chapter 10

REPORT FORMATS & STYLES

1.   The two basic formats/styles used to write police reports are: narrative and category.   T   F

2.   Special paragraphs are used in police reports to point out important information.   T   F

3.   The information in special paragraphs is usually technical and easier to understand in a separate paragraph.   T   F

4.   The following special paragraph is correctly written: T   F

Loss:

(1) Sony Model 2000 19" color TV, ser. #273461, with a black plastic cabinet

value: $100.00

(1) 14k gold woman's ring, with a 1 carat diamond mounted in a rose setting

value: $5,625.00

(1) Smith & Wesson Mod. 19, .357 cal. blue steel revolver with a 6" barrel and wood grips

value: $395.00

TOTAL LOSS: $6,120.00.

5.   The following special paragraph is correctly written: T   F

Evidence Collected:

1/2 (1) Igloo ice chest, 10 qt. size

2/2 (1) Clear plastic baggy containing approx. 13 ounces of marijuana

Deputy Walsh booked all evidence at the Sheriff's Department in evidence locker #4.

Chapter 11

CHECK LIST FOR CRIME REPORT NARRATIVES

1. Officers do not need to articulate their probable cause for stop, detention, and arrest.   T   F

2. When evidence is seized without a warrant, the officer must articulate his probable cause for the search and seizure.   T   F

3. The elements of the crime may or may not included in the narrative.   T   F

4. Depending on state law, there may be special circumstances that enhance the penalty for crimes. T   F

5. Specific modus operandi factors do not need to be included in the narrative.   T   F

Chapter 12

CORRECTIONS REPORT WRITING

Review Questions & Practical Exercises

1.   A report is a ....

2.   The purpose of the report is to ....

3.   Once a report is written, it becomes a ..... record and a ....

4.   Reports in correctional facilities fall into three different areas. They are:

1)   _____

2)   _____

3)   _____

5.   Name the seven essentials of a complete report:

1)   _____

2)   _____

3)   _____

4)   _____

5)   _____

6)   _____

7)   _____

6.   The seven essential elements are key to development of an accurate and defensible report. True / False

7. Name the five requirements of a report:

1) _____

2) _____

3) _____

4) _____

5) _____

8. The report must cover all details concerned with the incident or occurrence.   T   F

9. An outline is a good tool to use prior to writing a report to aid in conciseness.   T   F

10. Big words and investigative jargon are impressive in a report.   T   F

11. Record only the facts and make sure spelling and grammar are correct.   T   F

12   Courteousness and fairness reflect the personality and training of the writer.   T   F

13. A report is a formal presentation of facts.   T   F

14. The purpose of the report is to document any unusual incident.   T   F

15. Once a report is written, it becomes a permanent record and a legal document. T/F

Chapter 13

SUSPECT DESCRIPTIONS

1. Victims and witnesses are more likely to recall suspect descriptions if the officer conducts a thorough interview. T F

2. It is not important for suspect descriptions to be detailed and complete. T F

3. When asking a victim or witness to describe the suspect, try to start at the suspect's head and work down to his feet. T F

4. The race or descent of a suspect is used as an identifier. T F

5. During the interview of a victim or witness, it is better to ask generic questions, rather than specific questions about a suspect's clothing. T F

Chapter 14

SPELLING

1. Officers may keep a list of words they've spelled wrong in reports. This list is called a "speller's journal". T F

2. A speller/divider lists correctly spelled words and their definitions. T F

3. A thesaurus is a book of synonyms. T F

4. Proofreading by another officer or supervisor reduces spelling errors. T F

5. Homonyms are words that sound alike, have different meanings, and are spelled differently. T F

6. Spell out all titles except Mr., Mrs., Ms., Mmes, Dr., and St. (saint, not street). T F

7. Spell out Street, Road, Park, Company and similar words used as part of a proper name or title. T F

8. Spell out Christian names (William, not Wm.). T F

Chapter 15

PENMANSHIP

1. The use of a lettering guide doesn't help penmanship.   T   F

2. The use of traffic or crime scene templates improve penmanship.   T   F

3. The use of a portable typewriter may help officers improve the neatness of their reports.   T   F

4. Handwritten reports should be block printed in capital letters.   T   F

5. A larger barrel pen will help improve penmanship.   T   F

Chapter 16

GLOSSARY OF TERMS

1.　An adjective modifies a verb.　T　F

2.　An adverb modifies or describes a verb, adjective, or another adverb.　T　F

3.　A noun is the name of a person, place, or thing.　T　F

4.　A "doer" is the same as a subject in a sentence.　T　F

5.　A sentence is a group of words containing a subject and predicate and expressing a complete thought.
　　T　F

SAMPLE REPORT NARRATIVES

The following sample police report narratives are provided to assist officers in developing their writing skills and personal style. Police report writing is an art and not a science; therefore, there is no perfect report. Take the best from these samples and incorporate the best of your own skills to write good reports.

MINOR IN POSSESSION OF ALCOHOL

FACTS: You are on patrol in the county beach parking lot and arrest a minor for possession of beer.

Sample Report:

Evidence Collected:

1/2 (1) open and empty Coors beer bottle

2/2 (5) unopened bottles of Coors beer

All evidence was booked into evidence locker #6

When I drove through the parking lot of Salt Creek Beach, I saw Snow's car parked at an expired meter. I walked up to the car and saw Snow holding an open bottle of Coors beer.

She gave me the bottle, her drivers license, and registration, and then got out of the car. I found 5 more unopened bottles of beer, in an Igloo cooler, on the front seat of the car.

I read Snow her Miranda rights from my printed card. I asked if she understood and she said, "Ya, I understand." I asked if she wanted to talk to me and she said, "Ya."

Snow said it was her beer and that she got it from her boyfriend. He wasn't with her today.

I cited Snow for possession of alcohol and parking at an expired meter. I booked the evidence in Sheriff's Department evidence locker #6.

ASSAULT & BATTERY/SPOUSE ABUSE

FACTS: You are dispatched to a family disturbance call. Your investigation reveals the husband slapped his wife and she wants to prosecute.

Sample Report;

Evidence Collected:

1/1 (3) photographs of the victim's injuries

Evidence was booked into evidence locker #21.

On 1-3-90 at 1845 hrs., Officer Laughlin and I were dispatched to a family disturbance call. When we arrived we stood outside the apartment and could hear a man and woman arguing inside.

I knocked on the door and suspect Mr. Remender answered the door, however he only opened it a few inches. He said there was nothing wrong and he didn't need the police. We could see Mrs. Remender standing behind her husband. She was crying and motioned for us to come into the apartment. Mr. Remender opened the door and let us in.

Laughlin and I separated the Remenders and I interviewed Mrs. Remender first. She told me the following:

She was fired from her job today and as a result came home late. When she got home, she went to the kitchen and started to fix dinner. While in the kitchen, she argued with her husband. Mr. Remender accused her of having an affair with her boss. She denied the accusation and Mr. Remender became more angry. She said he finally slapped her, across the face, with the back of his left hand. After he slapped her, he left the kitchen and Mrs. Remender called the police.

Mrs. Remender said her husband had slapped her on two other occasions in the last six months, however she didn't file a police report. She said she was tired of his abuse and wanted him arrested.

I looked at Mrs. Remender's left cheek. Her cheek was red and swollen.

I interviewed Mr. Remender and he said the following:

He said they'd been having trouble for about 6 months. He thought she was having an affair with her boss and that's why she was always late coming home from work.

Initially Mr. Remender denied hitting his wife. When I told him she wanted him arrested, Mr. Remender admitted he slapped her. He said he slapped her one time using a back hand motion with his left hand.

I arrested Mr. Remender for felony spouse abuse. Officer Laughlin booked Mr. Remender at the county jail.

I photographed Mrs. Remender's injuries and booked the photographs as evidence in evidence locker #21. I also gave her a copy of the spouse abuse information brochure.

ASSAULT & BATTERY/PRIVATE PERSON ARREST

FACTS: You and your partner are dispatched to a call of two subjects fighting in the park. Your investigation reveals Mr. Watson punched Mr. Jones. Mr. Jones arrested Mr. Watson.

Sample Report:

Evidence Collected:

1/1 (2) photographs of the victim's injuries

Evidence was booked into evidence locker #12.

Today at 1245 hrs. Officer Moore and I were dispatched to a report of two men fighting in McFadden Park. When we arrived Jones and Watson were standing near the tennis courts and were arguing. Moore and I separated the two men and I interviewed Jones first.

Jones told me the following:

He was on his way to school, driving N/B on McFadden Blvd., when he noticed a fire truck parked at the curb by the park. The firemen were letting water out of the hydrant which caused a large puddle in the street. Jones said he passed the truck but didn't know it at the time, that when he drove through the puddle, water splashed onto the sidewalk.

Jones heard a man yelling and looked in his rear-view mirror. He saw Watson waving his arms trying to get Jones to stop. Jones pulled over to the curb and stopped his van. He got out of the van and walked to the rear to see what was wrong. When he got there, Watson punched Jones in the face. Jones said the punch was unprovoked and knocked him to the ground.

Jones showed me his broken glasses and a small cut on the bridge of his nose. Jones said he wanted Watson arrested. I explained private person arrests for misdemeanor crimes to Mr. Jones. He said he was willing to arrest Watson.

I approached Watson to interview him and he spontaneously said, "Hey, I shouldn't have decked him." Watson said he jogs in the park all the time and Jones was driving, "Like a maniac." He thought Jones drove through the puddle and splashed him on purpose.

I told Watson that Jones was going to arrest him for assault & battery. Watson said he understood and there wouldn't be any trouble because he'd been arrested before.

Jones arrested Watson for assault and battery. I handcuffed Watson and booked him at the county jail. I took photographs of Jones's broken glasses and the cut on his nose. I booked the photographs into evidence locker #2.

RESIDENTIAL BURGLARY

FACTS: You are dispatched to take residential burglary report. Your investigation reveals the crime has just occurred.

Sample Report:

Loss:

(1) white envelope, approx. 4"x12", from the Tropicana Hotel in Las Vegas, value: nil

U.S. Currency - (2) $100 bills, (2) $50 bills, (5) $20 bills, value: $400.00

(1) RCA 19" color TV, serial #416025, wood grain cabinet, value: $250.00

TOTAL LOSS: $650.

Evidence Collected:

1/1 (1) screwdriver with a standard head and yellow plastic handle

Evidence was booked into evidence locker #9

Victim Collins told me the following:

He locked all of the windows and doors to his home and left for work this morning at 0730 hours. No one had permission to be in his home. At 1200 hrs. he got a call at work from his neighbor Mr. Harding. Harding told Collins there was a suspicious person at Collins's house. Collins left work and arrived home at 1215 hours.

When Collins arrived he found the front door to his home open. Collins went inside and found the house ransacked. His TV was missing from a table on the West wall of the family room. He was also missing $400 in cash in an envelope from the Tropicana Hotel in Las Vegas. Collins kept the envelope and money in his bedroom dresser on the East wall of the master bedroom. Collins said nothing else was missing.

I checked the interior and exterior of the house for the point of entry. The sliding glass door to the master bedroom was open and there were pry marks on the door. I found a screwdriver on the patio outside the sliding door. I collected the screwdriver as evidence and photographed the scene. I booked all evidence into Sheriff's Department evidence locker #9.

I went next door and interviewed the witness, Mr. Harding. Harding told me the following: At approximately 1130 hrs. he was mowing his front yard. He saw a blue VW bug park in front of Collins's house. The suspect got out of the car, walked up to the Collins's front door, and rang the door bell. When no one answered, the suspect went around to the back of Collins's house.

Harding went inside of his house and called Mr. Collins at work. When Harding came back outside, the suspect and car were gone. Mr. Harding said he didn't recognize the suspect or car, but could identify them if he saw them again.

I called Identification Technician Garcia to work the crime for additional evidence. See her report for additional information.

I checked residences in the area for additional witness, but no one was home. I checked the parking lots of the local high school, park, and shopping center for the suspect's car and didn't find one that matched the description.

NOTE: The descriptions of the suspect and his car are not repeated in the narrative because they are included on the front of most crime reports, the face sheet. The same is true for the items taken, there is no need to repeat all of the description, it is already included in the Loss paragraph.

RESIDENTIAL BURGLARY

FACTS: You're dispatched to a residential burglary report. Your investigation reveals there is one witness to the burglary.

Sample Report: category style format

SYNOPSIS

Two suspects entered the victim's house and stole a stereo and TV. They did not have permission to be in the house or take the property.

SOURCE

On 7-25-89 at 1130 hrs. I was dispatched to a residential burglary report at 8132 White Street. I arrived at 1145 hrs. and spoke to the victim, Mrs. Brower.

SCENE

The victim's home is a single family residence in a residential neighborhood.

VICTIM INTERVIEW

Brower said she locked all of her windows and doors and left at 0730 hrs. to take her husband to work. She stopped at the market and returned home at approximately 0930 hrs. When she arrived home the front door was still locked. Her TV and stereo were missing from a table by the front window in the living room.

Brower said she found the kitchen door partially open.

OFFICER INVESTIGATION

The point of entry was through the kitchen door. I saw no pry marks on the door. The TV and stereo were taken from a table in the living rom. The living room was ransacked.

I checked the area and wasn't able to find the suspect's truck.

WITNESS STATEMENT

Ms. Jones lives across the street from the Browers. Jones said she saw a small yellow pick-up truck park in front of the Brower's house at about 0900 hrs. Jones watched the two men stay in the truck and talk for a few minutes.

Jones said the passenger, suspect #1, got out of the truck and walk into Brower's backyard. Suspect #1 walked out of the front door of the Brower house, carrying the TV. He put it in the back of the truck and then got back in the cab and talked to the driver.

The driver, suspect #2, got out of the truck and walked into Brower's backyard. He came out the front door carrying the stereo. He put the stereo in the bed of the truck.

Both suspect then went into the backyard. They both came out of the front door carrying stereo speakers. They put the speakers in the truck bed, got in the cab, and drove away.

Jones said she has seen the truck before, but couldn't remember where. She can identify the truck if she sees it again. She said she didn't recognize the suspects, but could identify them if she saw them again.

EVIDENCE

I called Evidence Technician Frazee to work the scene. She her report for additional information.

NOTE: The headings used in category style reports may vary from agency to agency. If your agency uses category style, be sure to check the department report writing manual.

ROBBERY

FACTS: You're dispatched to an armed robbery that has just occurred at Bob's Liquor Store.

Sample Report:

Evidence Collected:

The Identification Bureau, Technician Young, arrived at the scene for photographs, latent finger prints, and evidence collection. See Young's report for additional information.

Today at 1556 hrs. I was dispatched to an armed robbery that had just occurred at Bob's Liquor Store. I arrived at 1559 hrs. Store manager Gene Senecal met me in the parking lot.

He said that at about 1550 hrs. the suspect entered the store through the front doors. He walked to the back of the store and returned to the check-out counter with a bottle of wine. The suspect put the bottle on the counter, reached inside his shirt, and pulled a small shiny revolver from his waistband. He pointed the gun at Senecal and said, "Give me all the money."

Senecal opened the register, pulled out approximately $100 in various denominations, and placed them on the counter. Senecal said the largest bill was a $20 bill and he didn't take any coins out of the register.

The suspect took a Winchell's doughnut shop bag out of his right front pocket and put the money inside the bag. He left the store through the front doors and drove toward the freeway in a blue VW bug. Senecal said he didn't recognize the suspect or car, but could identify both if he saw them again.

Senecal said there wasn't anyone else in the car. He wrote down the license plate number on a piece of paper. I collected the paper as evidence and gave it to ID Tech Young when she arrived.

I interviewed the stock-boy, James Woods. Woods said he was at the rear of the store near the coolers when the suspect spoke to him. The suspect asked where the wine was and Woods pointed to the shelf. Woods said he only saw and spoke to the suspect for a moment and wasn't aware of the robbery until Senecal told him. Woods said he didn't recognize the suspect, but could identify him if he saw him again.

I called the Watch Commander, Lt. Brown, and requested investigation respond. The radio dispatchers issued a broadcast of the suspect's description and car at approx. 1557 hrs. I maintained the crime scene until ID Tech Young and Detective King arrived at 1645 hrs.

SAMPLE NOTES

```
Fri      Shift III       Area 329
Lt Rain     Lt. James - W/C
Unit 2031   Sgt. White - Field Sup

1705/1745              DR 04-19241
Burglary Report        333 Oak


inf/vic:  Collins, Wilbur Michael (3-9-55)
          WMA
          (H) 333 Oak St., Santa Ana 92777
          (714) 555-1234
          Elec Eng
Loss:     (1) RCA 19" color TV mod XL100
          Ser # 13579          $200
          U.S.  Currency
          (5) $20's
          (3) $100's            $400
          (1) Envelope - white legal size
          "Luxor Hotel, Las Vegas
          return address.        nil
          Total                 $600
```

Evidence -

    1/1 1/4" std screwdriver w/yello plastic handle

Collins

  0730   Left for work - house locked

  1200   Call from Harding

  1215   Arrived home

           Front door open

           TV missing from family room

           Money & envelope missing from dresser

           House ransacked

           Slider in master bdrm open, pry marks

           screwdriver on patio

Wintess:

           Harding, George Wm (11-30-52)

           WMA

           335 Oak St, 92777

           (714) 555-5867

           Retired firefighter

  1130   Mowing front lawn

           Suspect drove up & parked

           Went to front door

           Rang bell - no answer

           Went to rear of house

Harding went inside
Called Collins at work
Came out
Suspect & car gone

Car 70-74 VW Bug, lt blu, good condition, unk plate

ID Tech Wagner notified & arrived 1725; photo, prints, collect screwdriver

Patrol checked area - school & mall

Knocked on doors at 328, 338, 329, 339, 349

No one home

INDEX